NATHAN

CHILE
THE EXPAT'S GUIDE

An Insider's Guide to Living,
Working and Travelling in Chile

Table of Contents

Table of Contents

Chapter 1

Introduction

In November 2010, my business, Entrustet, was one of 23 businesses invited by the Chilean government to receive a US$40,000 grant to come to Chile for six months to be a part of Start-Up Chile's pilot round. Since then, I've lived in Chile for much of the past 6+ years building businesses, traveling, teaching in universities. Now I run Magma Partners, Chile's first 100% private early stage venture capital investment firm. It took me about a year to start to really understand Chile and many more to understand most of its nuances, so I decided to write the book I'd wished I'd had when I moved to Chile.

It all started in September 2010, when my business partner Jesse Davis and I were in our office in Madison, WI working hard on our startup company, Entrustet, dreading the start of the Wisconsin winter. We'd just graduated from the University of Wisconsin and were looking for a change of scenery. I saw an article in Forbes that said that the Chilean government was offering startups US$40,000 of equity free money to move to Santiago for six months, just when Wisconsin winter would be setting in.

We were excited, but a bit nervous. We didn't know anything about Chile besides that Santiago was the biggest city, Chileans liked soccer, they had good wine and fruit and they'd just rescued the miners (Wisconsin students' most popular Halloween costume in 2010).

We did research, talked to one other entrepreneur who'd already been accepted to Start-Up Chile and spoke to any Chileans we could connect with. We looked online for information, but didn't find much. After a bit of debate, we knew we had to take a chance... What's the worst that could happen? If it didn't work out, we could just fly back! In mid-November 2010, right as the first snow was falling in Madison, we packed up and took off for sunny Santiago. We had no idea what to expect.

We were part of the pilot round, arriving as the seventh company to participate in Start-Up Chile. It didn't hit me until I got off the plane and was waiting in line at customs that I'd be living and working in a foreign country for half a year. Our six months in Chile ended up being some of the best of our lives. We made lifelong friends both inside and outside of the program and got to know Chile on a personal level.

We grew our business, got press and tried out different business models. I even got to give a speech, in Spanish, in front of 200+ people including Chile's President, at La Moneda, Chile's version of the White House. During my six months, I not only learned about Chile, the country and its culture, but I also learned about myself. I had to figure out how to fit-in in a new culture, navigate new customs, learn a new language, all the while working with the stress of running a startup. Hopefully this book gives you a leg up so you have it easier than I did.

We left after six months, returned to Madison and continued to work. Nine months later, Entrustet was acquired and I decided that I wanted to finish learning Spanish while learning how to do business in the rest of Latin America.

I came back to Chile and worked with Welcu, a Chilean startup funded by US venture capitalists and successful Chilean entrepreneurs. A Start-Up Chile friend and I created a university class called *How to Build a Startup*, which we taught at Universidad Católica, Universidad de Chile, Universidad Católica del Norte and Universidad del Desarrollo over the next two years.

In the meantime, I helped prospective Start-Up Chile entrepreneurs get into the program by doing application reviews, getting a 60% acceptance rate, compared to the program's ~5-10% and started testing business models so that I could learn more about the market, including an ecommerce platform that helped me learn about the best opportunities for ecommerce in Latin American (Chapter XXX, Section 6).

By 2013, I realized that I was doing everything an investor does (mentorship, creating connections & deciding which entrepreneurs to work with) except actually invest money. I wrote a plan to create Chile's first and only 100% private seed stage venture capital firm and started to look around for potential partners.

As fate would have it, my Start-Up Chile experience continued to pay dividends. One of the founding team members, Diego Philippi, called me up and told me that he had been put in contact with a Chilean Family Office that wanted to invest in new businesses and was looking for someone to run it. Diego and I updated my original plan and then presented it to Francisco Sáenz, the head of his family office. After a few meetings, we started Magma Partners, the first Chilean/US venture capital firm and the only VC firm that uses it's partners own private capital.

After three years, in January 2017, we've now invested in 49 entrepreneurs from 28 companies (50% Start-Up Chile alumni) that employ 163 people from 17 countries on four continents. We invest in two niches:

B2B startups based in Latin America that sell to large Latin American companies.

Startups whose primary market is the United States, but have their technology team and/or sales back office in Latin America.

I wrote the first version of this book in 2012 to share what I learned with new Start-Up Chile entrepreneurs and am updating it in February 2017 to include everything that's changed since then.

You'll learn about what it's really like to live in Chile, Chilean culture, learning Spanish, the cost of living, how to find an apartment, doing business in Chile, how to find investors in Latin America, cultural differences, travel hotspots, favorite places to eat, drink and go out, and much more. After you read my book, you'll have a frame work for how to make the most out of your time here, whether you're staying for a few days or planing to stay for life!

Nathan Lustig
Santiago, Chile, 2017

SECTION 1

How to Read This book

I wrote this book to be used in conjunction with my blog, www.nathanlustig. com. I recommend you refer to it as a reference while you're reading this book as it contains the most up to date photos, maps and guides that will help you plan your time in Chile.

Feel free to skip around and read what's most important for you and your needs. If you have questions or feedback, please feel free to email me at nathanlustig@gmail.com.

Chapter 2

Chile at a glance

If you can only read one part of this book, this is it. This is the quick and dirty five-minute reference guide from what I've learned in Chile. I'll go into more detail as we move through the book.

1. Spanish

If you don't speak any Spanish, you'll survive and do fine, but being able to speak just a little bit will make your stay much more fun.

Enroll in a Spanish class in your hometown. Take another one when you arrive. Play with Duolingo. I regret not doing it. I got even more out of living in Chile once I started learning in earnest after my third month. I made friends with more Chileans and set up a weekly happy hour with a new friend to better learn Spanish. There are many more opportunities for enjoying yourself when you can at least understand what's going on and participate a little.

2. Where to live

If you're young and are not strapped for cash, live in Providencia between the Salvador and Tobalaba metro stops, Barrio Italia or in Lastarria and

Bellas Artes. Providencia is a little nicer, but Bellas Artes has been gentrifying since 2010 and is a cool, walkable place to live. These areas are close to the metro, walking distance from bars, restaurants, grocery stores. When I first lived here, I lived right by the Pedro de Valdivia metro stop. I wished I had lived about 2-3 blocks off of Av. Providencia, as it is much quieter.

The vast majority of apartments are managed by brokers who charge you 50% of the first month's rent upon signing a lease. You can find apartments yourself by looking online and you might find a non-managed apartment, but it's not likely. Since you'll likely pay a broker either way, I highly recommend working with a broker who is going to be on your side and specializes in helping foreigners rent apartments. ***Note: Two expats and I started*** AndesProperty.com, ***contact@andesproperty.com, to help hundreds of foreigners find great accommodations and avoid problems with Chilean landlords.***

If you find a good apartment, reserve it quickly; they fill up fast. You can live farther "up" (east, closer to the mountains) in Las Condes, but it gets more expensive and there are fewer things to do at night. El Golf to Alcantara metro stops, Chile's financial center and nicknamed Sanhattan, is expensive for what you get.

Farther "up" are more high-rise condos, around Metros Escuela Militar and Manquehue, but there's not much to do. These are good places for families or people who just want to work. Vitacura is good if you have a family or plan to work from home, but it's not close to the metro and is one of the most expensive places in the city. Houses are cheaper to rent, but there are hardly any furnished options.

It's a good idea to start looking for apartments before you get here. You can save time, effort and money by doing research ahead of time. Consider living with Chileans. A few of my friends did and this and ended up paying less rent, had friends right away and could ask their roommates questions when they were lost. Consider posting in the Start-Up Chile Facebook group, as alumni leave they have apartments to rent. ***Note:*** *You can also check out Andes Property, andesproperty.com, (*contact@andesproperty.com*) my furnished rental company.*

3. Exchange Rate

There are generally around 550 Chilean Pesos to 1 US Dollar and the Chilean peso nearly perfectly tracks the price of copper. If copper goes up, the Chilean peso gets stronger and vice versa. Since 2014, the Chilean peso has fluctuated between 600-700, making Chile less expensive for foreigners. To easily convert prices, double the first numbers and take away two zeros. For example, something that costs CLP$10,000, double it to CLP$20,000, then take off three zeros, making it $20. Since the peso is currently weaker, ~650 per dollar, I triple the CLP, $10,000x3=$30,000, then take off three zeros ($30) and divide by 2 ($15). It's not perfect, but it gets pretty close. Use xe.com for the best exchange calculations.

4. Internet

I have VTR high-speed Internet in my apartment and have used Movistar in our office. Most buildings only have one option, so you're likely stuck with whatever your building has to offer. Many buildings are only wired for a specific speed internet... so make sure to ask before you rent.

5. Make friends quickly

Get to know Chileans quickly, it will make your time in Chile much more fun.

6. Accept as many invites you can from Chilean entrepreneurs & friends

It's the best way to get to know the country and were some of the most fun times I had. I wished I had accepted more invitations.

7. At the Grocery Store

Cashiers will likely ask you two questions when you're checking out. First, they'll either say something like "club lider?" or "acumulas puntos?" which is their rewards points club. You can either say no or give them your RUT. You can use the points for discounts later.

If you pay with cash, they'll ask you if you want to donate the last few pesos to a charity. Say yes... even homeless people won't accept 7 pesos. Seriously! A guy gave my friend back the 1 and 2 peso coins and kept the 10-100s that he gave him. If you pay with a credit card, they will ask "cuotas?" which means "payments?". Say no o "sin". That just means you want to pay it all at once and your foreign credit card doesn't support cuotas anyway.

Look for a local produce store. It's 20%-50% cheaper than the supermarket and much higher quality. Plus, you're supporting a small business.

8. Arrival

When you first get here, walk all over the city to get to know the place. Stay in an AirBnB in Providencia, Bellas Artes or Bellavista to get acclimated if you haven't already rented an apartment ahead of time.

9. Taxis & Uber

Taxi drivers will likely try to rip you off. They probably got all of us when we first got here, but just always insist on the meter. Or better yet, take Uber, SaferTaxi (Start-Up Chile alumni) or Cabify (Start-Up Chile alumni). If the meter looks like it's going up too fast, just say no, get out and get the next taxi. Rates should be: $12-20k ($15-$25) from the airport to Providencia. Bellavista-Central Providencia $1500-2500 ($2-$4). Providencia to Vitacura, between $2-6k ($4-$12), depending on how far you are going.

Another sure fire way to make sure you don't get ripped of is to just get in, say your address with authority, then shut up. Then they don't know if you're a foreigner who lives in Santiago or a tourist. Or if you start to get comfortable, talk to the taxi drivers. They are usually interesting and are the best people to practice Spanish with. If you screw up, you'll never see them again and if you don't understand you can just stop talking. They also won't rip you off if you're trying to talk with them and say that you live here. I highly recommend using Uber or Cabify. It will make your trips much less stressful, and usually cheaper than taking a Taxi. If you do take a taxi, don't tip except maybe a 50 or 100 pesos to help with the change; it's not done in Chile.

10. Metro

The metro is your friend. It's easy, cheap and safe. Buy a BIP card (metro card) your first day here. A ride costs ~CLP$600 (US$0.90). Put CLP$5000 (US$7.50) on it and recharge as necessary.

11. Restaurants

They are fairly expensive for what you get. There are good restaurants here, but you have to find them. It's not like in NYC, San Francisco or even Madison, WI where you know that if you walk into a restaurant it's going to be good. I'll go into a long list later in the book. I regularly update my list on my blog: http://www.nathanlustig.com/2015/04/26/chile-restaurant-guide-best-restaurants-in-chile/

12. Take advantage of the ability to travel.

Go to Viña del Mar, San Pedro de Atacama, Pucón, Puerto Varas, Patagonia, Chiloé or neighboring countries like Peru, Argentina, Brazil, Colombia or Uruguay whenever you can. Buses are cheap, safe and excellent. Check last minute deals on LATAM or on Sky Airline for cheap flights around Latin America. Specials generally come out every Tuesday. Search in Spanish from the Chilean site, the prices are cheaper. Use your RUT to book instead of your passport if you can; you sometimes get better deals.

Be sure to not miss your LATAM flights or decide you want to change them. LATAM are really hard to deal with, especially if you've taken the first leg of a flight. Customer service is not their strong suit. You can pay more to have the option to change.

13. Eat Chilean seafood and Peruvian cuisine, drink Chilean Wine

They are awesome and the best culinary part about Chile.

14. Be Patient

Chile is known for conservatism and bureaucracy. Waiting in line for a paper to be stamped might as well be the national sport. You'll have to wait in lines and spend time on things that get done in the US in minutes. If you're patient, it'll usually work out.

15. Share your experiences

Whether you blog, tweet, Instagram, write on forums or keep a personal journal, share your experiences. Your family and friends will appreciate it.

16. Going out

If you like to drink, learn to like Pisco. It's most similar to brandy. Try pisco sours (pisco, lemon juice, powdered sugar) and piscola (pisco and coke). People eat late and go out late. If you go to a club before about 1:00, it'll likely be pretty empty.

17. Not much is open on Sunday

Only the big chain restaurants, big malls and a few of the grocery stores are open on Sunday. Many restaurants are closed. This is less true in Vitacura and Las Condes.

18. Enjoy every minute, it goes by way too fast

If you are here for a set amount of time, take advantage of every opportunity. It goes by way too fast. If you're moving here, take time to savor the ability to move abroad. Not many people have the chance or ability to do it.

Chapter 3

Chilean Culture

A country of a little over 16m people, Chile is Latin America's safest, most stable and most prosperous country. Nearly half of Chileans live in Santiago, and another 10% live in the Valparaiso area, an hour and a half drive west from Santiago, on the Pacific coast. There are six more cities with between 200,000-600,000 people, spread out over the entire country. The nicer parts of Santiago remind me of California, as does the rugged Pacific coastline.

If you put Chile on its side and put the top in New York City, Chile would almost reach Los Angeles. It's a long, skinny country with different ecosystems and geography in each region. From the hot coastal cities of Arica and Iquique in the far north to the netherworldly landscapes of San Pedro de Atacama, to La Serena and Valle del Elqui north of Santiago, down to Santiago, Viña del Mar and Valparaiso, to Pucon and Temuco, Puerto Montt and finally Patagonia all the way at the bottom. The south is extremely beautiful, quiet and natural and has a heavy German influence and great food.

Lose the movie version of South America. Chile's been a safe, stable democracy with multiple power changeovers since the late 1980s, when democracy was restored after Augusto Pinochet's military dictatorship. There are no kidnappings of foreigners, gun battles in the streets, drug gangs or major organized crime issues. In areas where most foreigners will be, Chile seems very close to a first world country. Parts like Vitacura, Las Condes, La Dehesa are very much like the US, while parts like Bellas Artes, Lastarria, Barrio Brasil and others are like Europe, complete with sidewalk cafes, plazas, metro, cabs, busses and the ability to walk around. There are certainly areas that are unsafe, just like any other major city, but Santiago and Chile in general seem safer than any other Latin American counterpart.

Chile generates nearly $19,000 in GDP per person, the highest in Latin America, but it is distributed very unequally. Nearly 80% of Chileans earn US$800 a month or less. Much of Chile's wealth comes from copper: it produces 33% of the world's annual output. Chile also exports wine and fruit all over the world. Chile is almost always rated as South America's best place to do business: there is little to no governmental or police corruption, it's fairly easy to start a business and there is a strong rule of law. The recent uptick in price fixing scandals and political influence peddling are a black mark on an otherwise mostly clean country and while terrible, are nowhere near as severe in size and scope as other Latin American countries.

The summers from Santiago northward are long, warm and dry. It can get up to 37C in the dead of summer, but quickly cools down each night. It's dry and if you are out of the sun, it's not too bad. The winters are short and temperate. It rarely snows in Santiago. At night it can get as low as -3C, but during the day it normally rises to about 15C. It's cooler and wetter the farther south you go from Santiago, and the coast can be windy and raining, especially in winter.

Santiago has a pollution problem that can be a problem for young kids or the elderly. It's especially bad in winter where Santiago has some of the worst air quality in the world. I have mild asthma and it hasn't really bothered me, but other friends have complained about the air quality in certain areas. You can see it when the mountains get obscured by the smog or by the dirt that accumulates when you leave a window open.

As a foreigner, you'll find a beautiful, safe, laid-back country and a great quality of life. Sometimes if I go to a café in Providencia and have my headphones turned way up, I'll forget I'm in Chile and not Palo Alto.

Chileans have a sort of European attitude to life, but with a South American twist: they want to work and get things done, but not too hard. There's an incredible amount of bureaucracy, but that's starting to change. When I joke that the national sport is tramites, getting papers stamped by the correct people, I'm really not far from the truth. Chileans really value family, asados (BBQ's), weekend get-aways, keeping up appearances, and vacation.

Compared to other large national capitals, Santiago is fairly inexpensive and offers great quality of life. Santiago has poor areas, but it doesn't have the sprawling slums of Brazil or India. Real estate prices have risen very fast over the past five years, leading some to speculate that there is a bubble in certain parts of the city.

Chile is a traditional, Catholic, family oriented country that is very divided by a rigid class system. Foreigners from the US and Europe likely won't be subjected to classism. In fact you may even benefit from it. But if you pay attention you will see it. It took me three months to start to see it, but nearly a year to really understand how deep it goes. This is my least favorite part of living in Chile. You'll also have to deal with conservatism and bureaucratic companies and governmental agencies. Things generally work out in the end, but it takes longer than you think it should.

Chile and its neighbors have a peaceful, but strained relationship. Chile won wars against Peru and Bolivia in the 1870-1880s, which resulted in Bolivia losing its only access to the ocean and Peru losing billions of dollars of minerals that Chile now exploits. Bolivia still disputes its turn of the century peace treaty and demands access to the sea at international summits. There are hundreds of thousands of Peruvian and Bolivian immigrants who do mostly menial, low wage jobs and many Chileans look down on them. Argentina and Chile have a rivalry and don't like each other too much either, but relations are getting better.

Santiago is a large, up and coming city. It's the only South American city in the top 10 fastest growing cities in the world. While it doesn't have the history or culture of Buenos Aires, there are tons of fun things to do and there are plenty of benefits to living in Santiago. It's a great place to live and work and I'm confident you'll have a great time if you come here either as a tourist, student or long term resident.

SECTION 1

A brief history of Chile

Chile has been inhabited for at least the last 12,000 years. There are multiple Native American cultures throughout Chile including the Mapuches, Araucanians and Aimarans who populated Chile before Spanish rule. The Mapuches were strong fighters who held off the powerful Incans, the Native Americans from present day Peru, for hundreds of years. The first European to see Chile was Ferdinand Magellan in 1520, but the first European to actually come to Chile was Francisco Pizzaro's partner, Diego de Almagro in 1537. Chile didn't have the natural mineral wealth that Peru, Mexico or other Spanish colonies had, so it was relegated to second or third class status. Spanish nobles wanted to go where the money was, so Chile's Spanish rulers were generally younger sons without fortunes. Chileans sometimes half jokingly/half seriously say that their country got the runts of Spain.

In 1541, Pedro de Valdivia decided that he wanted to expand the Spanish empire and invaded Chile, defeating the northern Native Americans and founding Santiago. Cerro Santa Lucia, now a public park, was Santiago's first outpost. Although there wasn't much gold or silver, Chile had vast natural resources like arable land, fresh water and access to the sea. But the expansion came at a cost. The Mapuches fought against the Spanish and

even to this day were never fully brought under Spanish rule. According to Chile's national history museum, it took until 1880, seventy years after Chilean independence, for the Mapuches to be "subdued." Between the lack of natural resources like gold and silver and a ferocious resistance by the indigenous people, Chile was not viewed as particularly interesting for Europeans and was one of Spain's poorest colonies.

In 1810, the Chilean upper class split into two. Criollos, Spanish descendants who were born in the new world, fought a brutal civil war against each other. One side wanted to stay part of the Spanish empire, while the other side wanted independence. Although it was an upper class fight, indigenous and mixed race lower class people were usually the people actually fought. After seven years of war, Bernardo O'Higgins, known as "the Liberator", and Jose de San Martín massed an army in Mendoza, Argentina and invaded by crossing the Andes. After defeating the Spanish in 1818, San Martín continued north to expel the Spanish from Peru. O'Higgins became the supreme leader and ruled until 1823, while the war was still going on. The war lasted until 1826 when the last Spanish soldiers were kicked out of Chile.

From 1830 until 1861, a conservative government, marked by a strong executive and a weaker Congress, promoted business and stability and won foreign wars. Unlike O'Higgins, this government received more support from the Catholic Church and business leaders. Although at the beginning it was somewhat democratic and liberal, it deteriorated into a de facto dictatorship with Diego Portales, a government minister, running things behind the scenes. Although Chile's economy grew, it was at the expense of some freedoms. Wealth became even more concentrated into the hands of an elite few.

Although the government was still under the watchful eye of the powerful landowners, things began to change in 1861 as the central government became stronger. In 1883, Chile defeated Bolivia and Peru in the War of The Pacific and incorporated the northern third of modern day Chile into the country. This war still has significant repercussions today. The war eliminated Bolivia's access to the sea and took some of the richest deposits of saltpeter, at that time used to make fertilizer and gunpowder, and the richest deposits of copper and gold, which today account for a massive percentage of Chile's wealth. Bolivia still stokes anti-Chilean fervor whenever anything goes wrong and blames lack of access to the ocean as the principal reason for its underdevelopment. Chile, Bolivia and Peru still have strained relations from this war in 1883; the map of South America would look very different if the war had a different outcome.

In 1886, Jose Manuel Balmaceda was elected president, but during his term he became more conservative and ended up as a dictator. Congress acted to try to blunt his power and there was a civil war, which resulted in Balmaceda's defeat. The new regime limited presidential power and handed it to landed elites and representatives in Congress. They used bribery and payoffs to control the country, but otherwise allowed for dissent, civil liberties and at least the appearance of democracy. There were elections and stability, but the country's economy was fairly dependent on nitrate exports. During WWI, when the Germans invented synthetic gunpowder, eliminating the need for nitrates, Chile suffered an economic downturn and reformers began to get more power.

By 1924, the middle class started to press for new power to control the country. They elected Arturo Alessandri Palma, who was the first Chilean politician to take his campaign directly to the people. He started to reform, but was blocked by the conservatives in Congress. There was a series of coups and dictators over the next eight years before the left leaning Radical Party won power and increased state power in the economy. In the 1960s, a fairly moderate President, Eduardo Frei Montalva, began to push through education, housing and agrarian reform, but the Left thought it wasn't enough and the Right, too much.

In 1970, Salvador Allende, a member of the Socialist Party, won a plurality of a three way presidential election. Allende won with 36%, followed by the conservative candidate at 34% and then another leftist candidate at 27%. When there's a plurality, the Chilean Congress gets to choose the president and voted in Allende. The Allende government wanted to nationalize parts of the copper industry, increase land reform, increase workers' rights and work more with "people's republics" around the world. The US, partly to protect business interests and partly because of the anti-communist fervor of the time, put economic sanctions on Chile and according to declassified CIA documents, the CIA began to try to "instigate a coup to prevent Allende from taking office."

Allende nationalized banks and intervened in natural resource companies, while at the same time increasing workers' rights and spending on public works projects. He froze prices, increased wages and changed the tax code.

It all seemed to be working for the first year, but in the second year, there was massive inflation, up to 140%, and capital flight. The US was not happy with Soviet Union intervention in Latin America and the nationalization of US company interests and under Henry Kissinger's direction began to "make the economy scream" by funding CIA operations, imposing embargoes and trade sanctions.

On September 11, 1973, the military staged a coup with CIA backing. The military bombed La Moneda, the seat of government (the Chilean version of the White House) and took over the country. Allende killed himself, rather than be taken alive. Augusto Pinochet, the commander of the army, seized power shortly thereafter and became dictator. At least three thousand people were killed or disappeared during the dictatorship and tens of thousands more were tortured. 30,000 people left the country. In a 1988 plebiscite, Chileans voted to restore democracy, which led to presidential elections in 1989 and the 1990 restoration of democracy.

During his dictatorship, Pinochet abolished civil liberties, free press, got rid of all of Allende's reforms, banned collective bargaining and imposed a curfew. The dictatorship followed the Chicago School of economics and privatized nearly everything and opened up markets. Inflation fell from 1000% to 10% and the economy boomed. All of this was going on with a backdrop of limited civil society, institutionalized torture, murders and "disappearances". In 1988, Chileans voted 54.4% to 45.6% that Pinochet should leave office at the end of his term and that Chile should return to democracy thereafter.

The dictatorship is still a very sore spot for Chileans and still colors politics and many parts of daily life. There are multiple narratives about the dictatorship and it completely depends on who you ask. For example, the main street in Providencia was called 11 de Septiembre until 2015 when the first non-conservative mayor was voted in, in commemoration of the day when the military overthrew the government. People still call Chilean states or regions "region 1" "region 2" etc, the names that the dictatorship used, instead of by their previous names like "lakes region" or other more common names. There are still political figures that played roles in the dictatorship who are in positions of power today. The 2013 presidential election pitted Michelle Bachelet against Evelyn Matthei. Matthei's father was a senior figure in the dictatorship, which Bachelet's father was "effectively tortured to death."

There are still people who fully supported the dictatorship and even the methods that were used. They claim that we were not there and cannot judge the military's actions. They say that if it weren't for Pinochet, Chile would be Venezuela or Argentina, with a President like Hugo Chavez or Cristina Fernandez. The other end of the spectrum holds that Allende would have made socialism work and that the dictatorship ruined the world's chance to see a functioning socialist government.

It seems to me that at least a plurality, and maybe even a majority or Chileans, believe that Pinochet's dictatorship saved Chile's economy and set the stage for having the best economy in Latin America today and the highest standards of living, but that the methods were wrong. It's still a touchy subject and I'd suggest that it isn't something to bring up with people you don't know. And if you do bring it up, it's best to listen, ask questions and actually try to understand their opinion. A friend's father was a police officer who carried out the dictatorship's wishes, her uncle was in the military and another uncle was tortured by the dictatorship. If even some families can't get on the same page, it's still a complicated area to wade into.

The Concertación, a generally center left coalition party, took power after Pinochet was forced out and held power until 2010. Michelle Bachelet, a Socialist, was Chile's first female president in 2006. In 2010, Sebastian Piñera, a center right businessman, took office, the first person from the right to hold power since Pinochet. Piñera has modernized the country and pushed for diversification of the economy, but has critics on the left, especially in education. Since 2006, there have been frequent, mostly peaceful, but sometimes violent, student protests pushing for free universal education. After going to the Museo de La Memoria, Chile's dictatorship memorial museum, and watching dictatorship era videos, many of the scenes from the protests look a bit like protests during the dictatorship. Clearly, they are not and freedom of speech and expression is allowed, but the dictatorship still casts large shadow on Chilean politics and culture.

In 2014, Michelle Bachelet won a second term and is currently serving again. Her government has been marred by self inflicted wounds from corruption and incompetence and external problems like a low Copper price, which has led to a weak economy. Chile is still primed to be one of Latin American's best countries and the economy seems to be straightening again.

SECTION 2

Chilean Culture

I've spent 6+ years in Chile, working and interacting with people in all levels of social and socioeconomic status. There are many differences between Chilean and US culture, some of which I love, others of which have been hard to get used to. Clearly not all Chileans are alike, but I believe this chapter paints an accurate picture of a typical Chilean you'll meet during your time in Chile.

Chile is a conservative, family oriented country that is fairly open to foreigners. This conservatism permeates most aspects of Chilean culture: working, politics, dating, marriage, gender roles, gay rights etc. Nearly everyone is Catholic, but many people are non-practicing. Although they may not go to church, they seem to fully believe and the vast majority have conservative attitudes. Every major Catholic holiday is a feriado, a day off of work, and most of the stores are closed.

Abortion is illegal under any circumstance; birth control is harder to come by than in the US/Europe, the morning after pill was prescription only until 2015. Many pharmacies still demand a prescription, even though it's

not required anymore. Divorce just became legal in the 2000s and men just recently are required to pay child support for children outside of wedlock. It's a macho country where gender roles are very defined and men are strong willed and many expect to be in control. Up until 1984 women were legally considered the man's property after they got married. Domestic violence is a significant problem, with 34% of women reporting physical abuse, nearly double that of the US.

Chileans generally live at home until they get married and have very close relationships with their families, especially their mothers. Although this is changing slowly. It's very common for the entire extended family to get together for lunch on Saturday or Sunday. Families are generally larger than in the US and it's not uncommon to meet people with multiple siblings, especially in the upper class. While upper class families are generally big, with up to eight siblings, the birth rate is only 1.8, the lowest in Latin America. Chileans, especially men, are very proud and don't like to admit they are wrong, which can lead to some funny arguments at asados (BBQs).

Chile is very class stratified, meaning the classes don't mix much. When two Chileans meet for the first time, they generally ask each other the basic interview questions: last name, where they went to university, where they went to high school and who's related to whom. It's like a measuring stick to see how they stack up, a way to place the other people in the society. If you look closely, it's almost the same ritual as two dogs meeting each other for the first time!

A Chilean will know someone's class just by looking at them and if you pay attention, you'll be able to differentiate fairly easily too. Note: when I'm talking about class, I'm talking about social standing, not good manners. You can probably boil down most class differences to how dark skinned someone is, although most Chileans won't admit it. You'll likely hear the word flaite, which basically means low class. The closest concept in the US is white trash, in the UK probably chav. Every class uses the word flaite to describe people below them. Much of the lower class has a deep distain for the upper class and many use the word "cuico" as a pejorative against the upper class. It goes both ways.

In the US, we have about four classes: the super rich, the fairly wealthy, middle class and poor. They are large bands and most families wouldn't think twice if a fairly wealthy daughter married a well educated, solidly employed middle class guy. In Chile, that likely wouldn't happen. The classes don't mix. They are physically and emotionally separate. Upper class Chileans' interactions with lower class Chileans are mostly in service situations or boss-employee relationships, which leads to more cultural misunderstandings.

The upper class doesn't mix with the middle class, the middle doesn't mix with the lower. Most upper class Chileans would never seriously date someone outside of their class, even if they're smart, educated and good looking. I went to a friend's birthday party that took place on the rooftop terrace of his apartment building. He invited three groups of friends: foreigners, upper class Chileans and middle class Chileans. Nobody mixed. The upper class group formed a circle with their backs to the rest. The middle didn't try to talk to the upper. And the foreigners sort of chatted. After a few drinks the upper class guys came over to hit on the other two groups of girls. It was a microcosm of Chile.

The country is very politically divided. Sebastian Piñera, elected in 2010, was the first conservative president since the dictatorship and during his tenure there were frequent marches pushing for better education. Michelle Bachalet, the president who both preceded and followed Piñera, is a Socialist and part of her coalition is very left leaning. Political polarization has gotten even more pronounced as Bachalet has tried to reform taxation, education, workers rights and write a new constitution. The upper class go to expensive private schools and the rest have to settle for a poor public education or spent 15-25% of their family income on a private school starting in kindergarten.

Chileans are generally private people and tend to worried about their status, especially in the eyes of their peers. They generally behave completely differently inside and outside of the house or when they are away from their group of friends. There's a phenomenon called the vacation effect, which means that people have fewer inhibitions away from home than in their own city. In my experience, the Chilean vacation effect is the strongest I've ever seen.

Women, be prepared to be whistled at in the street, especially if you have blonde hair. Chile is a very machista country and men get away with behaviors here that would land them with sexual harassment lawsuits in the US. Most men believe these behaviors are completely normal. For example, many of my Chilean female friends have been sexually harassed by bosses, coworkers or people in authority. Doesn't matter if they're dating, married, etc, it happens.

Men make comments in the workplace that are straight out of Mad Men in the 1950s USA. They might see a good looking woman walking toward them on the street, wait for her to pass, then stop, turn around and look at her for a few seconds before going on with their day. Although Chileans will make comments, it's fairly safe for women to walk around at night in Providencia and Las Condes, but they should be careful in other areas of the city, just like you would in any big city in the world.

It's not that Chilean men don't respect women, they do. The majority of Chilean men treat their mothers, girlfriends and wives well. They just believe that's the right way to treat women and that women like it. Although I don't condone many of the comments and behavior I've seen in offices, on some level, I think many Chilean women do like it to some degree, even if they won't admit it. They've just been raised in the macho culture and believe ogling and doing things that most people from the US would find demeaning is well within their rights, and that on some level that women like it. The macho latino is alive and well in Chile.

Chileans love BBQs and relaxing with friends and family. But it's not a BBQ like we have in the US with burgers, individual steaks and side dishes. A Chilean asado starts with choripan, chorizo sandwiches with mayo, mustard and sometimes onion. Next comes a huge chunk of meat that gets slow roasted on the grill for 1-3 hours. When it's done, the person in charge of the BBQ adds salt and cuts the big chunk into little pieces that get passed around to everyone.

Chileans drink copious amounts of piscola, the national drink, and enjoy relaxing and partying. It's especially true around the fiestas patrias, September 18th. A typical night out starts around 1030pm with a "pre" or a pre party in someone's house. You'll drink a few beers, have some piscola and then head out to a bar or a disco around 1am. Be careful, the laws changed in 2012 to make it illegal to drive with a blood alcohol level of .03 or higher. The penalties are draconian (starting with 6 months with no license), but it reduced road deaths by 80% the first weekend the new law was implemented. There's no excuse to drink and drive in Chile. Uber and its competitors are everywhere and much less expensive than in the US.

Chileans smoke like chimneys. The official stats say that 40% of Chileans smoke, but it sure seems like it's way more. In the US, it's about 20%. It's very normal to see young kids lighting up outside the metro or on the street and asados are filled with people smoking. Unlike the US, where smoking goes down significantly with education, highly educated Chileans seemingly smoke as much as their lower educated countrymen.

Cigarettes are still really cheap, as low as US$2.50 per pack. In 2013, Chile passed an indoor smoking ban that has made most restaurants and bars so much more enjoyable. They've also forced smokers outside, so if you're sensitive to smoke, know that you may be completely surrounded by smokers if you're eating outside. It seems to be somewhat popular to try to quit smoking now, but it's still a massive problem. Things seem to be changing. I organized an asado for the students in the class I teach and when it came time to light the grill, we couldn't find a lighter. Not a single person in the group of 27 smoked. It should be in the Guinness Book of World Records for most non-smoking Chileans in the same place at the same time!

Another big difference you'll notice: street dogs. They're everywhere, especially in smaller northern cities like Antofagasta and Calama and southern cities like Pucon. Unlike our image of street dogs in the US, these dogs are mostly calm and like people. They seem to be mostly well fed and many will actually refuse to eat bread, preferring to wait for meat. The only exception to their friendliness is if you're biking or jogging, you might find a dog that wants to "play" and will charge at you barking. If you don't get scared, you'll be ok, unless you get flustered and fall off your bike. But you never know, you might just run into a stray that's the exception to the rule.

Many people don't take kindly to "gringos" or people from the US saying they're from "America." It's offensive to some, a joke to others and completely innocuous to the rest, but it's sure to raise a debate if you ask. In the US, most of us refer to our country as America and ourselves as Americans without a second thought. Growing up, we just assumed that's who we are. It's used offhand every day by millions of people. Virtually every Presidential address in my lifetime has begun with "my fellow Americans." It's part of our culture.

Before I got to Chile, I already knew that some people found it offensive that people in the US have appropriated America to refer only to the United States because I had learned about it in a Latin American studies class in college. But I assumed that it was mostly overly politically correct people. I was pretty clearly wrong.

Once I got here, I realized it was more widespread than I thought. Everyone seems to have an opinion. Some Chileans don't care at all and refer to the US as America and its citizens as Americans without a second thought. Others playfully pointed out that they too were Americans and others were actually offended. I'd say that most were in the middle. They'd prefer that the US didn't call itself America, but weren't really offended. Some examples:

I was at an asado and a Chilean friend of mine asked a girl where she was from. She said America. He responded with a smile, "oh yeah, me too." He told me he loves to do that, mostly as a joke, but partly to make the point to people from the US that they are not the only ones from America. Another friend cringed when I said something about America to refer to the US and corrected me. He wasn't offended, but said it grates on his ears when someone from the US uses America that way.

The new US startup program is called Startup America, which is especially galling to some in Chile, as the program is basically a knock off of Startup Chile, but appropriates the name of the entire hemisphere. Another friend posted a video by Alfredo Jaar video called "This is Not America" on her Facebook wall and got 100+ likes, 20+ shares and 15 comments in one day!

I've also seen many Chileans mostly playfully turn the globe "upside-down" so that Chile is at the top. The most southern province, Magallanes, even has its official symbol with Antarctica at the top of the map, not the bottom. From my view there is only a small group on the far left that is truly, deeply offended by the term American, but there is definitely a large group of people who would prefer that people from the US didn't say American to describe themselves. It grates on them, but it's not a huge deal to them.

In Spanish you say estadounidense, but in English there just isn't a word other than American. I've pointed this out many times, and I think the best response came from one of my Chilean friends. She said something along the lines of "you guys took the name, you gotta come up with something to replace it." So sometimes I jokingly say I'm Unitedstatesian.

In 2015, I wrote a blog post about Chilean culture. For two weeks after I published, nothing happened. It was just like any other blog post. But on a Sunday evening, I posted it on social media and went to sleep. I woke up the next morning to a full email inbox and a crashing blog. My post had gone viral and would be translated into Spanish (poorly, as sensationally as possible) and would be viewed more than 1,000,000 times over the next week and be discussed on national radio and tv. I'd get angry emails, personal attacks and even some death threats! It's still one of my top trafficked blog posts and generates an email or comment weekly.

What caused such a furor? My post called *The Best Thing a Chilean Can Do Is to Leave Chile*. I mean it with an implied "and come back", but since there's three ways to translate "leave Chile" in Spanish, the media choose the most drastic, which meant, "leave and never come back," leading to the post's extra virality. I hope it will give you a window into Chilean culture. If you're interested, check out the original on my blog to see the more than 450 comments to get an idea of how Chileans reacted. Enjoy!

SECTION 3

The Best Thing A Chilean Can Do Is To Leave Chile

After five years in Chile, I firmly believe that the best thing a Chilean can do to better his or her life is to leave Chile. Traveling is ok, but to get the full benefit, a Chilean should live and work abroad, ideally for at least a year. Working in another Latin American country is ok, but to get the full benefit, a Chilean should try to live and work in the US, Europe, China, Japan, Korea, Australia, New Zealand or another well developed country with a completely different culture and set of values. It's easy to see the difference in attitude in a Chilean who's been abroad and one who hasn't.

Both upper class Chileans and non upper class Chileans should leave Chile, but for different reasons. For non-elite Chileans, their lives get instantly better getting out of Chile's classist system. They instantly have more opportunity, are more likely to get evaluated for who they are, how smart they are and not their skin color, where they went to school or their last name. Non-elite Chileans quickly realize that lighter skin and blonde hair isn't always aspirational in every part of the world.

They find lots of people who actually prefer darker hair and features and find them more attractive than traditional northern European features.

When I talk with non-elite Chilean friends who go abroad, they tell me that smart, educated, motivated non-elite Chileans find both their platonic and romantic prospects much improved and I would imagine self esteem has to go up. Their prospects for success go up the moment they step off the plane. They have the chance to see that if they work hard they might actually be able to better their lot in life. After being abroad for awhile, many non-elite Chileans don't come back for a long time, unless they have to. And many of the ones that do, have a different view on what's possible.

Upper class Chileans should leave Chile to break down many of the attitudes they've grown up with. Many (if not most) upper class Chileans are overtly classist and nearly all are unintentionally classist. Many, if not most, don't mean it maliciously, but do it subconsciously.

Leaving the Chilean bubble where life is easy, people live at home until they're in your mid 20-30s, have a maid and don't have to worry about much, is a wakeup call that shows that the rest of the world really doesn't have it like you do. Upper class Chileans generally don't interact with non upper class Chileans, expect in service situations, so really getting to know people from different backgrounds, who think differently and don't come from the bubble builds empathy and understanding for others that they likely wouldn't run across if they stayed in Chile. Leaving the bubble forces them to recognize their privileged lifestyle and gain a degree of self awareness that many elite Chileans are sorely lacking. (Many times, you see a similar effect from sheltered suburban kids in the US).

They see that (shockingly!) white people do manual labor in some developed countries. That some people find dark skinned people more attractive than lighter skinned people. They see that rags to riches stories are valued in other parts of the world and not looked down on as they are in Chile. They are given the opportunity to recognize that maybe Chile isn't the best country in the world at everything. And that's ok.

Both upper class and non upper class Chileans should leave Chile to see what it's like to live in a society where service is excellent, people trust each other and are generally nice to each other in day-to-day interactions. They can see that being passive aggressive isn't the route to success. That asking for things directly is probably the best way to get what they want. That saying no to things they don't want is much easier than saying yes to everything when they really mean no.

They learn to be more independent and not to always be able to rely on their parents getting them out of jams well into their 20s. It gives them a chance to raise their expectations for Chile so that when they come back home, they have a new attitude about what is possible, what is right and how they want to live their lives. By far the best thing a Chilean can do is to leave Chile. At least for a year or two.

Note: I think the best thing someone from the US can do is to leave for a few years too, but if a US citizen doesn't leave, the downside is much less than if a Chilean never leaves.

Edit to add: December 14th, 2015: This post went very viral and I've said this in the comments probably 20 times, so I'm adding this here. The biggest misinterpretation of this post in the last line, the note. Many are taking it to mean that I think the US is better than Chile. I'm not saying that at all. My entire point is that the US is much bigger, has more immigration, more tourism, more universities where you leave your comfort zone, different kinds of people in different cities so that your chance of meeting someone different from you is higher if you never leave the US compared to someone who never leaves Chile.

SECTION 4

Elite Chilean Ambition

I wrote this article as a companion to The Best Thing a Chilean Can Do is to Leave Chile. It goes into greater detail why opportunities can be hard to come by in Chile.

One of the biggest things I've noticed working and living in Chile over the past six years is that most Chilean elites have a very different attitude toward business than US business people do.

In the US, most business people, even those with vast fortunes, are extremely driven. Whether they're driven to make more money, to get more recognition or more power, to make the world a better place, or for their own entertainment, most US business people are always looking for the next challenge. They want to expand, to try new things, to make more money.

If they own the 5th biggest mortgage business in the US, they're likely working their ass off and are very motivated to try to grow to #4. If they own the second biggest Honda dealership in the greater Milwaukee area, they're doing everything they can to get to #1. And they're busting their ass every day because they know people with smaller businesses are gunning for their spot. And so are new entrants into the market. US business people are generally extremely ambitious because they both fear competition and want to grow to make more money, leave a legacy or just because they enjoy it.

ambition

/am-**bish**-*uhn*/ *noun* - an earnest desire for some type of achievement or distinction, as power, honor, fame, or wealth, and the willingness to strive for its attainment

CHILE: THE EXPAT'S GUIDE

In the US, we celebrate rags to riches stories. We love to hear stories about people who came from humble beginnings to start massive companies, became doctors, lawyers, teachers or other success stories. We even celebrate just going from not having money to having money. We see it as a virtue in and of itself.

The typical Chilean elite attitude is very different. There aren't many rags to riches stories in Chile and people don't really celebrate existing stories. In many cases, many Chilean elites actually look down on people who came from the bottom to become successful. It's the opposite of the US.

The vast majority of Chilean upper class business people are all about preservation and extraction. The #3 pharmacy isn't going all out to be #2. The 5th biggest bread brand isn't busting their hump to be sure they aren't caught by the 6th. They're happy with what they have, making their share of the profits each year. They're not concerned that a new entrant will start to compete and take away market share.

Why doesn't competition scare them?

First, Chile has been isolated from the outside world for the vast majority of its existence. Chile is a small country geographically, isolated at the end of the world, so when foreign companies want to go into a South American market, they usually choose bigger, sexier markets like Colombia, Mexico, Brazil and Argentina first.

When foreign brands decide they want to come to Chile, they don't find it attractive to enter the market and compete directly. Instead, they mostly sign exclusive representation deals with Chileans, in effect, giving the representative a license to print money. In larger countries like Brazil, Mexico and Colombia, more foreign companies set up their own operations to make money directly, many times with lower margins.

Second, industries are highly concentrated into maybe a few hundred very wealthy families that mostly went to the same elementary, middle and high schools, and then onto the same universities. Everyone in the elite is one to two degrees of separation away from each other. Competing really hard against a family friend, a friend of a friend, a member of your church, or golf club is looked down on and most people don't do it.

Sometimes this lack of competition leads to direct price fixing, which happens with impunity, as the social and economic punishments are very low and price fixing isn't a criminal offense. When three large Chilean companies were accused of price fixing toilet paper and stealing US$37M by taking advantage of the poorest Chileans, Chilean elites didn't lead the outcry demanding justice and denouncing the families who run the companies. Some did, but the vast majority didn't.

Third, most Chileans don't have the resources or education to actually compete. 95% of Chileans make less than US$1400 and 85% make less than $900, 50% make minimum wage of US$310 and the vast majority of the "have nots" don't have a good education. You can't compete with a large-scale business if you don't have a good education or the ability to save a nest egg.

Finally, Chilean bureaucracy makes it much harder to start a business than it is in the US and requires up to 6-9x the startup capital as it does in the US because large Chilean companies pay invoices net 90-150, which means a new business owner needs 6-9 months of startup capital, whereas US standard net 30 payment terms means you need 1-2 months of startup capital to get going.

Why aren't elites motivated to grow?

If you're not afraid of losing market share from strong international competition, a new upstart or someone already in the market, you're more likely to be happy with what you have.

Most Chilean elites have a very good life. If you're a business owner, you likely have a nice house or apartment in Vitacura or La Dehesa, a house at beach enclaves in Cachagua, Zapallar, Maitencillo, a house in the mountains to go skiing, a chunk of land in the south with a beautiful house on it and maybe even an apartment in Miami or some other nice place.

And if you don't own them, your extended family or close friends have access to them and invite you along. Many have live in maids who make life easier. If you have the good life and aren't worried about competition, why would you be motivated to try to expand and make more money, optimize and make things better? Why not just let the machine run, collect profits and live the good life?

I can't say that I fault the elites who have this mentality, but ambitious people are the ones that change things, who make the world a better place, who help lift the world out of poverty, who discover big scientific breakthroughs and move the world forward. Right now, the vast majority of elites think that the good times will run forever. Copper will keep being valuable, the 85% of the non-elites will be happy with cheap material goods and won't demand a bigger share of the pie. I think they're wrong on both counts.

If Chile really wants to be a world-class country, it must find a way to motivate its upper class to be more ambitious, make the system better and easier to navigate for ambitious lower and middle class people to thrive or import foreigners who are driven and want to create new value. Otherwise Chile will sit with the status quo, extracting copper, making massive profits on capital, banking, property, agriculture and natural resources and 85% of its population will be unhappy, wanting to get into the middle class, but not being able to, creating a risk of left wing governments like Argentina or Venezuela that we know don't work.

And when (not if) copper is replaced by synthetic substitutes like Graphene or technological advances make copper less necessary for infrastructure and other manufacturing processes, the Chilean miracle will be over. When. Not if.

If Chile wants to be a world-class country, it must do better. And entrepreneurs from outside the elite will play a big part in making this future possible.

SECTION 5

Dating and Relationships

Chile is a conservative country with very traditional values and gender roles. There's a marked difference between dating in the US and many parts of Europe and dating in Chile. Most women want much more contact than their US counterparts do and expect more formality if you are at all serious. Abortion is illegal and very taboo, the morning after pill became available over the counter in 2015, but can still be hard to get in many pharmacies. Moral of the story: use birth control.

If you're at all serious about dating a Chilean woman, you have to formally ask her to be your girlfriend (pedir pololeo) and do it fairly soon into the relationship. I didn't realize this until I'd been in Chile a long time. Unless you say these magic words, your relationship isn't formalized. It was quite a shock coming from the US where if I'm seeing a girl for a few months and I ask her "will you go out with me? or, "I want you to be my girlfriend", she'll likely either laugh and think I'm incredibly cheesy. Or it could lead to a fight along the lines of "are you serious, what do you think we've been doing for the past month or two?"

Chilean guys strongly pursue girls they like. Men have a very intense style that pairs with many women's attitudes on gender roles. Most Chilean women play games and the guys play right along. It's a dance, an art form that I'd never seen other places I've travelled and I still don't quite get 100%. I have friends who have broken up and gotten back together 10+ times, something that's much more common in Chile than in the US.

Many Chilean women are very indirect. Nothing is clear-cut. It's "maybe" then yes then no, then maybe. Many men seem to enjoy it. Many of the things that women appreciate in the US are the exact opposite of what a Chilean girl wants or responds to. All of these cultural differences can be difficult and can lead to cultural misunderstandings!

Most unmarried Chileans live at home, so it's quite common to see couples making out in the park, on the metro, on the bus, just about anywhere. For a country with otherwise conservative values, it's striking. Walk through any park in Providencia or Lastarria during summer and you'll see what I mean.

Note: if you're from the US or parts of central and northern Europe, you'll notice that Chilenas are very warm and open once they get to know you a bit. It doesn't mean they want anything more than friendship, although it can. Chileans greet each other with a kiss on the cheek and hugs, there's much more touching here than in the US. Once you get used to it, it's very easy to spot friendly vs. interested, but don't get confused at the beginning or it could be awkward.

It can be very frustrating especially in the beginning, but as you learn, it starts to make sense. Dating outside of your culture is an incredible learning experience and one that, if you're single, you'll quite likely enjoy. You just may have to break down a bunch of barriers to get there. And it goes both ways. Most of my male Chilean friends are not very skilled at dating women from the US/UK, as it's just a completely different culture. The challenges go both ways!

Why Is Chilean Customer Service So Bad?

Over a two-week period, I went to three restaurants in Santiago that had incredible customer service. I was so surprised by good service that I had to compliment the waiter at each restaurant and got to talking with each one. What did they have in common?

One was Uruguayan, one was Peruvian and the other was Venezuelan. The Uruguayan waiter told me that he makes about 80% more in tips than his Chilean coworkers because he's nice to people and tries to go the extra mile. The Peruvian waitress was so nice, warm and got everything right and said that she couldn't understand why service was so much worse in Chile than in her home country. The Venezuelan waiter was incredibly attentive and got everything right. His Chilean partner gave zero fucks, forgot parts of the order, disappeared for long periods of time and added two extra items to the bill.

Chilean customer service is the worst I've experienced in all my travels. I've been all over South America, North America, Europe and parts of Africa and the Middle East and Chile is clearly the worst. I haven't been to Asia yet, but even if it's bad, which I don't think it is, Chile would be near the bottom of the barrel.

Customer service is bad in restaurants, retail stores, banks, service businesses, government offices and when you call the help lines. Imagine the experience calling Time Warner or Comcast, US Cable and Internet providers known for terrible customer service, and multiply it across all industries in Chile.

At restaurants, about 20% of the time the bill is wrong. I always order a glass of tap water and it only comes about 40% of the time, even after I ask for it multiple times. The waiters can't be bothered to bring me something that they won't get a tip on. Have a question about the menu? The norm is grunts and no real advice. I probably get a bit of hair in my food at once every three weeks and the normal reaction is barely an apology. Many times you'll see waiters hanging around talking and not bothering to help clients when diners clearly want something. I'd say I get actually good service at a Chilean restaurant about 30% of the time, bad service at least 50% of the time and 20% is just average.

Retail is worse. Employees generally act like you're bothering them if you want to buy something. And if you want to ask a question? Your answer will generally be short and in a tone of "why are you bothering me?" I've walked into stores with the intention of buying something, but nobody was willing to help me so I just walked out.

Try calling a customer service help line. These are generally bad in most countries, but Chile takes the cake. For example, awhile back I called my bank to ask a question. The representative asked for my details to look for my account and I asked my question. As soon as she realized it would be a hard question where she would have to work, she started to say "hello? Are you there? I cant hear you! hello! hello!" until she hung up. I was in my office where I have perfect reception. She just didn't want to work.

Most customer service reps will say whatever they can to get you off the line as quickly as possible, regardless of what they are saying has any basis in the truth. My rule of thumb is to call until I multiple people have told me the same answer.

It's frustrating coming from the US where good customer service is table stakes for a successful business. You might say it's the difference between a first and third world country or that it's a Latin American problem, but that's not right either. Argentina, Uruguay and Peru have incredible customer service. People are nice, generally knowledgeable and even if they can't help you, are happy to be trying. Brazil, Bolivia and parts of Colombia have some problems, but workers are generally happy and try their best. They're willing to bend the rules to help you out, whereas Chile has a rules are rules mindset.

So why is customer service so bad in Chile? And can anyone do anything to make it better? I believe Chile has a perfect storm of problems that create a cesspool of frustrating customer service.

First, the incentives aren't aligned and the people who have the power to align the incentives have no incentive to align them.

Chilean employers generally rule through fear, not through positive incentives. Employers might just fire a bunch of random employees just to keep the remaining employees on their toes. And in most jobs, it's nearly impossible to move up or get a significant raise. You might work your entire life making minimum wage, with little or no room for advancement. Real training in non-existent and management treats most employees as replicable inputs.

At restaurants, you pay a 10% fixed tip no matter the quality of the service. If service is really bad, you can try to give less, but if you're paying with credit card, you need to tell the waiter to his face that you don't want to tip him, which leads to confrontations, so most people just tip anyway. Studies have shown that countries that have the best service either have a completely variable tip, like the US, or no tip what so ever. In countries like the US, waiters are motivated to work hard to make big tips. In countries that don't have tipping, waiters are treated more like professionals and doing a good job is the expectation.

Most people blame the workers, and to some degree it's their fault. But the majority of the blame goes to the misaligned incentives. They are generally poorly paid, don't have tipping incentives to do a better job, generally poor working conditions and have to operate in workplaces ruled through fear. The best employee isn't going to earn much more, if any, than the worst one. And when you see the impunity that the elites have, you're not going to be motivated to give them good service if they walk into your establishment. If you think you're getting screwed, and you probably are, why bother?

Government Bureaucracy

Government bureaucracy is bad pretty much anywhere in the world, but I've seen things in Chile that would make waiting in line at the DMV look like a piece of cake. I was at the International Police getting a certificate I need for my permanent residence visa. The worker got a Whatsapp message that he "needed to answer" and spent the next five!! minutes planning his weekend while I was standing there and a huge line of people were waiting. Once he finally decided to process my paperwork, he'd spelled my name wrong and we had to start from scratch.

At the Chilean IRS (SII), the bureaucrats enjoy messing with the gringo. I needed to show SII that I had purchased products that I would sell before they would give me government receipts that allowed us to legally sell our product. The bureaucrat told me that my purchase orders would not be approved. I asked what more I needed to do and he said I needed more purchase orders. I asked how many more and for how much money, as I would easily go and get it. But he couldn't even give me an order of magnitude. He just didn't want to work. It's so frustrating!

After five years, there's not much you can do but laugh. And give extra big tips and extra compliments and gratitude when you get really good service. It's the first thing I notice when I travel to the US or Argentina.

SECTION 7

Food and Drink

Chilean Food and Drink

One of the most important parts of a country's culture is its food and drink. A good meal helps you discover a country both through the food and your dining companions. Chile is sort of like the US in that it doesn't really have a national cuisine, but has an amalgamation of different cuisines. If you love seafood and meat, Chile is the country for you. It has some of the best fresh seafood in the world. If you're a vegetarian and like to cook, Chile is an incredible country, but most restaurants are not really veggie friendly. Between seafood and Chile's incredible produce, you can eat really well in Chile, although the vast majority of restaurants are mediocre at best. Ironically my favorite "Chilean" food is Peruvian food. Here's a list of some of the most common foods you'll find in Chile.

Chilean Food

Chile is known for seafood, barbecues and has very few traditional dishes. The food in Santiago is generally pretty poor at restaurants; you have to

search out the good ones. See Chapter XXX for my complete guide. Although they'll profusely deny it, Chileans generally don't like spicy food. If you go to a restaurant and like spicy food, you'll need to ask for extra spice. The servers, alarmed, will think you're nuts, but just tell them not to worry. Here's a list of some of Chile's most popular dishes:

Cazuela – Cazuela is a soup with clear broth that has potato, squash, corn on the cob and a big hunk of meat. Can be made with chicken, beef or pork. Sometimes it has other vegetables or rice mixed in. It's great for a cold winter day.

Pastel de Choclo – Cornmeal casserole baked in an earthenware dish filled with beef, chicken, hardboiled egg, olives, raisins, onions and other vegetables. Another winter staple.

Machas a la parmesana – Chilean sea clams on the half shell, covered with Parmesan cheese and cream, then baked in the oven. Incredible with white wine.

Lentejas – Lentils cooked with rice. A typical proportion is 95% lentils and 5% rice. Served piping hot.

Pebre – Pebre and bread come with nearly every Chilean dish. It's the staple like bread and butter is in the US. Pebre is made of tomato, chopped onions, cilantro and aji (Chilean hot peppers).

Caldillo de Mariscos – A fish and seafood stew, served mostly on the coast.

Choripan – A staple of an asado (BBQ), a choripan is chorizo+pan (sausage and bread). A Chilean BBQ will start with a few choripanes then move onto bigger cuts of meat. Served with mayo and mustard. Sometimes avocado.

Humita – Similar to a Mexican tamale, it's cornmeal, onions, fresh corn and sometimes meat cooked in a corn husk. You can either eat them with salt or with sugar, but not both.

A lo pobre – Any Chilean meat dish can be served "a lo pobre" or "like a poor person" and it comes with french fries, onions and a fried egg or two. Great when you're really hungry, but not the healthiest choice.

A lo macho – Covered in a creamy sauce with a mix of seafood. Mostly found in Peruvian restaurants.

Crudo – Raw ground beef served with lemon juice, aji and a yogurt based sauce served on toasted bread.

Curanto – A stew made with every seafood you can think of, plus sausage, beef pork and potatoes. It can be cooked in a hole in the ground in a pot. Specialty in southern Chile, especially Chiloé.

Mote con Huesillo – Sweet peach iced tea with dehydrated peaches that are rehydrated via the sweet iced tea with freshly cooked wheat kernels. It's a dessert, but you can buy it on the street on a hot day for a refreshing treat.

Chupe – Stew that can be made from nearly any protein source, but the most typical is chupe de mariscos (assorted seafood).

Marraqueta – The most common Chilean white bread. It comes in 4 small rolls that are connected together. It's great for sandwiches, or toasted for breakfast.

Empanadas – Chilean empanadas come in three main varieties that can be baked or fried. First, pino, which is ground beef, raisins, onion, black olives (with the pit, be careful) and hard boiled egg. These are common all over Chile, but less common on the coasts. Second, seafood, which can be any type of seafood and a bland white cheese. Third, plain cheese. A good empanada is a delicacy, but a crappy one is like a McDonald's hamburger.

Parrillada – A mix of meats served on a small wood burning grill that's brought to your table. Meant to be shared by at least two people.

Chorrillana – A huge pile of french fries covered in beef, chicken fried onions, egg. Meant to be shared. Best accompanied by beer.

Completo – Chilean hotdog with avocado, mayo, tomato, onions and more. Can be served "Italiano" with tomato, mayo and avocado (like the Italian flag). Chileans eat the most hotdogs per capita of anyone in the word, most of which are cheap, crappy filler hotdogs.

Ceviche – Sometimes spelled cebiche, is raw seafood and fish "cooked" in lemon juice with onions, cooked corn and a side of pumpkin. The acid in the lemon juice cooks the seafood over the course of 4+ hours sitting in the fridge. Incredible, especially on the coast.

Aji – Chilean hot pepper.

Merken – Condiment made from dried and roasted hot peppers. The quintessential Chilean spice. I use copious amounts in most of my cooking.

Manjar – Dulce de leche in the rest of the world, it's a sweet caramelized spread for bread and cakes made from condensed milk.

Palta – Avocado. So good.

Wine, Spirits and Beer Wine

Chile has world-class wine for bargain basement prices. You reliably pick any wine that costs more than $3500 (US$7) in a liquor store or grocery store and find something pretty good. If you spend $5000 (US$10), you'll be virtually guaranteed something really good. You can get a good bottle of wine at a restaurant for $7500 (US$15), so be sure to take advantage of it. I drink more wine while I'm in Chile than when I'm in the US. I really don't know much about wine, so my heuristic for finding a good bottle at the liquor store is to feel the indent on the bottom of the bottle. The deeper it is, generally the better the wine. It seems to work in about 80% of cases. Chile's signature wine is Carmenere, a deep red wine, and most any variety of Chilean wine is worth tasting.

Spirits

Pisco – Chile's national liquor. It can be between 70 and 90 proof (35 degrees and 45 degrees as the Chileans say it), and is made from grapes. It's most similar to brandy. You almost never drink it straight. Alto de Carmen and Mistral are the two most common decent brands. ($3000, US$6 in the liquor store) If you want to go cheaper, go for Capel.

Pisco Sour – Aperitif that packs a stronger punch than you'd think. It's piscso, lemon juice and sugar. The Peruvian version has raw egg white and bitters. Both are served freezing cold.

Piscola – Chile's national drink is piscola, pisco and Coke mixed together with ice cubes. Chileans make their drinks strong, sometimes 50-50 or even stronger.

Piscola Blanca – A piscola but made with sprite or ginger ale.

Terremoto – Sweet white wine, fernet (a strong clear liquor), and a dollop of pineapple ice cream. Sweet, gut rotting drink that will knock you on your ass after 1-2. La Piojera is their birthplace.

Beer

Chileans don't drink much "good" beer, preferring to drink weak pilsners similar to Miller in the US. The most common are Escudo and Cristal. The craft beer scene is growing fast, here's a few of the most common ones:

Kuntsman – One of Chile's good craft breweries. Torobayo is my favorite.

Kross – A new craft brewery. I love their stout.

Austral – Larger craft brewery. Calafate is my favorite. See Chapter 12 for a list of bars with great beer lists.

Coffee

Chileans don't drink much real coffee, mostly Nescafe instant. If you're a coffee fan, you'll have to go to Starbucks or one of the few independent coffee shops that have real coffee. Generally your best bet is to go for espresso, as more places have real espresso machines. If you're a coffee fan, you're going to have a bit trouble in Chile. An enterprising Chilean entrepreneur wanted to increase coffee's popularity and created "café con piernas" or "coffee with legs" where you can drink coffee that's served by women in short skirts (or less, depending where you go). Since 2014, more small coffee shops have popped up in Bellas Artes, Barrio Italia and parts of Providencia.

SECTION 8

Natural Disasters

Chile is the most active seismic zone in the world. Chileans don't even consider earthquakes below 7.0 to be real earthquakes, using the term "temblor," a tremor. Anything above a 7.0 is a terremoto (earthquake) and anything below is just a temblor. The Pacific plate is smashing up against the continent and has been for thousands of years. It's created the Andes Mountains, which run like a spine from Colombia, down through Ecuador to Peru and down the entire length of Chile. Although Chile and Argentina share a massive land border, the Andes were nearly impenetrable, until airplanes made the trip quick and easy, thanks to the history of earthquakes and movement of the Pacific plate.

Because of these massive forces, Chile has an earthquake (temblor) somewhere nearly every day. Most of these earthquakes are tiny and nobody feels them, but every once in awhile, you'll feel one and every ~30 years, there's a massive one. In 1960, Chile experienced a 9.5 earthquake, the strongest ever recorded in the history of the world. Don't worry too much; Chile isn't due for a big one for a while.

In February 2010, an 8.8 earthquake struck Chile, throwing the country into chaos and killing 500+ people and leaving most of the country without power for 24+ hours. Fortunately, Chile is right up there with Japan for the best earthquake proofing technology and only a few large buildings in Santiago collapsed. Some smaller, older buildings didn't fare as well and neither did Southern Chile, which wasn't so lucky and suffered significant damage, leaving around 500,000 people with severely damaged or destroyed houses. There was a massive tsunami that destroyed thousands of homes and killed hundreds of people. As a result, Chile is installing a tsunami early warning system to help detect tsunamis as they happen. Tsunamis generally happen in tandem with large earthquakes and there are tsunami escape routes clearly marked in all tsunami danger areas. In 2016, more then 1m Chileans evacuated beaches on a holiday weekend in less than an hour after a strong quake triggered the new early warning system. The evacuation was a massive success.

The South has many volcanoes, but they're not dangerous in your day-to- day activities. Chile generally gets advanced warning when a volcano is going to be active, so when one erupts it causes mostly property damage. The Villarica volcano near Pucon puffs smoke most days and is very active, but again, there's an early warning system that should help keep people safe. There's a warning in the center of town that shows volcano danger in the form of red/yellow/green stoplight. The biggest inconvenience when a volcano is erupting is that it can interrupt air travel if the wind is blowing the right direction.

Chile has only one poisonous creature, the araña de rincón, the corner spider. These spiders are dangerous and hide in clothes, books, behind couches or other dark places. In three years in Chile, I've seen only one araña de rincón and many of my friends have never seen one in their entire 25+ years on the planet. You should be on the lookout and just know that they exist in case you come across a black, skinny-legged spider. If you get bitten, go directly to the hospital, as the venom kills your skin. If it's not treated quickly it can require amputations to stop the spread. I wouldn't worry too much, but they're worth knowing about.

Chapter 4

Getting to Chile and Getting Situated

O nce you've been selected and decide you want to come, you have to get your visa, book your flights and get yourself to Chile.

LATAM, American, United and Delta offer direct flights to Santiago from NYC, Dallas, Miami, Atlanta, Los Angeles and Houston while Air Canada has direct flights from Toronto. You can get cheaper but longer flights via Panama on Copa or Aeromexico via Mexico City or Avianca via Bogota. From the US you should expect to pay between $900-$1500. British Airways flies direct from London, Iberia from Madrid and Air France from Paris.

If you are really hard up for money, consider flying into Lima, South America's hub and taking a bus overland into Chile. It's 30+ hours from Lima to Santiago and I don't think it's worth the money you'd save unless you are REALLY on a budget. You can also fly directly to Lima, Sao Paulo, Rio de Janeiro, Buenos Aires or Bogota and then get an internal flight on LAN. Or another, sometimes cheaper alternative, is to take a bus from Buenos Aires across the mountains into Chile. I don't really recommend it unless you're doing it as part of a sightseeing trip and make stops at different towns in between.

The most expensive flights into Chile are in February, Chile's national vacation month and around Christmas, New Years and the Fiestas Patrias, Chile's Independence Day celebration around September 18th.

Travel Hack: if you have British Airways miles and are flying from the US, you can use them to fly to Chile on LATAM and American. Because BA doesn't fly from the US to South America, you can pay as low as 17,500 miles for a one-way ticket instead of the 30,000-50,000 you'd have to pay directly via American or Delta.

Travel Hack: If you're short on cash, or just want to explore other Latin American cities, check out booking a round trip from Santiago-Mexico City, Santiago-Bogota, Santiago-Medellin, Santiago-Lima and then a round trip from your stop over city to your destination in the US. You can usually find discounted routes by booking separately and it gives you an excuse to discover other Latin American cities. You can also negotiate 24-48 hour stop overs in most cities where you would otherwise have a short layover. Sometimes you need to call the airline directly to make the booking, but you can see another city for no extra charge.

Chile is a long, thin country of 3200 miles (5150km) long and only about 177km/110miles wide on average. Santiago is the capital and has about half of the country's population. This massive city generally runs from the mountains in the east toward the coast in the west. It is completely surrounded by mountains, which in winter leads to problems with smog. It's easy to orient yourself. Anytime you are lost, look for the tallest mountains, the Andes. That's the east. Remember, mountains, east. People talk about "going up" or "going down" when giving directions. East, toward the mountains, is up, west, away from the mountains, is down.

Cerro San Cristobal is a huge hill with a Virgin Marry statue on its summit just north of Providencia and Bellavista. You can use it as a good way to figure out North vs. South. Alameda (aka Av. Bernardo O'Higgins) is the main drag in the center of the city. Going up, (east) at Plaza Italia (Metro Baquedano), it changes to Avenida Providencia.

In parts of Providencia, Avenida Providencia spits into two parallel one way streets, Nueva Providencia going up, Providencia going down. As you cross into Las Condes at Tobalaba, Providencia becomes Avenida Apoquindo and continues up. In Vitacura, which is north and east of Providencia, Avenida Vitacura is the main street.

Santiago is very safe and nice pretty much anywhere above (east)

Baquedano and north of Bilbao, plus Lastarria, which is closer to Santiago Centro. Bellas Artes, areas in Santiago Centro and Ñuñoa are safe as well, but parts can be a bit sketchier at night if you're walking alone. Other areas of Santiago are ok as well, but I'll go into more detail later in the book.

Travel Hack: Chileans have a strange habit when you ask for directions. Even if they don't have any idea of how to direct you to where you're asking, they'll still give you directions and sound incredibly confident. When I first got here, I asked for Diego de Velasquez 2071, a little street just off of Nueva Providencia near the Pedro de Valdivia metro stop, one of the biggest streets in the city. The guy didn't know, but he told me that I had to go 20 blocks south, that's where it was, he was sure. I knew he was wrong and didn't go out of my way and found the street I was looking for right around the corner.

Chapter 5

Getting Around Santiago and Chile

Most of Santiago is very accessible via public transportation. Santiago's bus and subway system are unified under one government agency: Transantiago. You purchase a BIP card at any subway station or from one of the many stores or kiosks in the city. Busses don't accept cash, only your validated BIP card. I usually put 5 lucas (1 luca=$1000 pesos=US$1.50) on my card, which is good for about 8-10 rides depending on peak usage. Chileans complain it doesn't work, but it's one of the best public transport systems I've seen and far better than any in the US, except maybe NYC.

The metro runs from 630am until 11pm except on Sunday when it closes at 1030pm. Busses run 24/7, but slow from one every 5-7 minutes to once every 30 minutes late at night. Santiago has a very modern, clean and efficient metro that costs between CLP$500-CLP$600 (US$0.75-$1) per ride, depending on peak hour usage. Busses don't stop at every bus stop, even if people are waiting so make sure to put your arm out as if you were flagging a cab and the bus will stop for you.

A bus and subway ride cost the same price and you get free transfers from the metro to the bus, bus to metro, and from one bus route to another for two hours after you first swipe your BIP card. You can save money by taking the metro to a meeting and then take the bus back. It's a flat rate to go one stop or 20.

Colectivos, or shared taxis, are cars that run on prescribed routes throughout Santiago. You share them with up to three other people. They cost a flat rate between CLP$300-CLP$2000 (US$0.50-$3), depending on the route. You flag them down just like you would a taxi and pay the flat rate as soon as you get in. When you want to get out, you simply tell the driver and he'll pull over for you. They are safe and much faster and more comfortable than taking the bus, while much cheaper than taking a taxi or Uber, especially for longer trips. They usually run from places not served by the metro and are one of my favorite ways to get around.

Taxis are very prevalent in the main parts of Santiago where you'll likely hang out. While they are generally safe, fairly cheap and easy to use, I highly recommend Uber, Cabify or EasyTaxi so that you can be sure you're not getting ripped off. Many taxi drivers like to try to pull one over of foreigners, so use Uber if you can. It's actually cheaper than taxis. Although they're still not fully legalized, you don't run into problems. Make sure to help the driver out by getting into the front seat when you get into your Uber.

Taxis costs CLP$250 (US$0.50) to get into a taxi, then CLP$100 (US$.20) for every 200 meters you travel. It's cheap. If you go on the highways, you're responsible for the TAG, or the metered tolling. A fare from the airport to the center should be $10,000-$13,000 (US$14-$20), Providencia a bit more. You should never pay more than $17,000 (US$30) from the airport to the Center, Las Condes, Providencia or most parts of Vitacura. If you are going from the airport and don't want to take Uber, negotiate a rate from the taxi counter before you leave baggage claim. They won't screw you as badly as the individual taxi drivers waiting outside. If you need to go from Santiago to the airport, you can use Transvip, a shared bus service. Call ahead and they'll pick you up at your door and take you to the airport for $6,000 (US$12) per passenger. There's also a bus that goes from the airport to metro los heroes for about $2000 (US$4). Uber is roughly $13.000 from Providencia.

Taxi drives love to screw foreigners. Their favorite tricks include not turning on the meter, turning on the meter so that it moves more quickly than normal and giving you incorrect change. The best way to avoid these tricks, other than taking Uber, is to authoritatively say the street you are going and then shut up. That way they don't know if you're a tourist or a foreigner who's been living in Chile forever. You can also use Google maps to get a route and track your progress until you're comfortable navigating Santiago. If you notice the meter going up too quickly or the driver going off route, tell the driver to stop, get out and either pay a nominal amount like $1,000 or don't pay at all. Get a new taxi, or switch to Uber.

Taxi drivers know most of the main streets, but not the small ones. They will also pretend not to know somewhere and take you for a ride to try to screw you if they think you're a foreigner. You can always ask them to use Waze or Google maps. Be careful, be confident, and be decisive and you won't get screwed. Don't ever get out of your taxi before making sure you have all your possessions: bag, phone, wallet. Always check the seat as you're getting out before you close the door. If you leave anything behind, you're not getting it back.

For travel between cities, busses are inexpensive and safe. Buy from bus ticket depots or directly at the main bus stations or online from startups like Recorridos or PasajeBus. Be sure to take an express bus if you are traveling between cities, as you will save hours. I still have flashbacks to a 16 hour local bus ride from Pucón back to Santiago instead of the 9-10 hours on the direct bus. It's worth the extra 25-50%. You can fly between cities in Chile fairly cheaply using LATAM and Sky airlines. Look for specials. Overnight flights are generally the cheapest.

Renting a car is an option for getting around in Chile. A small car should cost about between $15,000-$25,000 (US$25-US$45) per day. It's better to call a company if you speak any Spanish, as you will generally get a better deal than going online. Look for local alternatives rather than the international companies. Like bus tickets, cars generally are tough to get for long weekends unless you reserve in advance, but otherwise are very easy to come by. You generally only need your foreign driver's license and a passport to be able to rent, but you're supposed to get a Chilean driver's license after being in Chile for 3 months.

If you're going to be in Chile longer or you can think about buying a car. Cars are more expensive than in the US and gasoline is very expensive, just like in Europe. Gas is currently US$1.74 per liter or US$6.60 per gallon, which the average price per gallon in the US is US$3.60. I get around without a car, but rent a car or borrow a friend's when I need to travel long distances or run big errands. Avoid rush hour, there's terrible traffic during the morning and evening commutes.

Chapter 6

Cost of Living

Overall, Santiago is a fairly inexpensive city for a world capital. Although there has been a property boom from 2009-2015, which have seen real estate prices in prime areas rise up to 300%, it's still not too bad. Some things are much cheaper in Santiago, while other are much more expensive. Comparisons are loosely based on prices in Chicago, a moderately priced large US city, not New York or San Francisco, which are outliers.

Cheaper

- Unfurnished apartments and houses, especially 10 minutes walking distance or more away from a metro stop or outside Providencia, Las Condes, Bellas Artes (as low as US$500/month)
- Taxis/Uber
- Services like maids, cleaning people, handymen, shoe shine etc (US$20 for a complete house cleaning)

- Fresh fruit, vegetables, wine, seafood especially if you shop in small shops rather than the big box stores (50% less)
- Drinking... if you drink Pisco, wine or local beer (US$7 for a bottle of pisco)
- Cigarettes (US$4 per pack)
- High end restaurants (very good value for money)

About the same

- Furnished apartments close to the subway
- Low end restaurant meals (but generally lower quality than in the US/Europe)
- Metro and bus rides
- Airfare

More Expensive

- Electronics (~20%+)
- Brand name clothes (50-100% more and poor selection)
- Printed books (bring a kindle)
- Drinking (if you're drinking imported liquor or craft beer, 30-50%)

I lived well on $1500/month and can get by at even $1000 if I really need to. At $1500 a month, I was eating at restaurants ~3 times a week, going out 1-2 times and generally living well and enjoying myself. Since 2014, as the currency has devalued, Chile has gotten much more affordable.

Cell Phones and Internet

There are three main cell phone companies here in Chile: Entel, Movistar and Claro. People seem to generally prefer Entel, but Movistar and Claro are decent bets, too. Virgin Mobile and Wom are recent entrants into the market and are on the Movistar network. The vast majority of Chileans (85-90%) use prepaid phones.

If you have an unlocked smartphone, I highly suggest a Virgin Mobile Anitplan or a similar plan from Wom. They're the best value for money, and not coincidentally, foreign owned. You can also find someone to unlock your smartphone at one of the many small shops in Santiago Centro.

If you want to purchase a phone in Chile, you can find a cheap smartphone phone for $20,000 (US$20) and you're good to go. You put $5,000-10,000 ($10-$20) on your phone and you can use voice and texting until you run out. Recharging is very easy and can be done in a kiosk, the grocery store, an ATM or one of the girls in the metro station. You just need to tell them your company and your cell number and you're recharged.

Unlike in the US, texting is very expensive compared to voice. On my old prepaid account, I could talk on the phone for 1.5 minutes for the cost of one text message. Incoming calls and texts are free. Pretty much everyone uses Whatsapp for messaging.

For internet, VTR and Movistar are likely your two options. Each high-rise building has been cabled by one or the other of these companies. You don't have a choice, you just need to hire the one that's in your building. A decent connection will cost $25,000 ($50). You may need to have a RUT to get internet access, so either rent a furnished apartment that includes internet, or ask your landlord to sign up for internet in their name. Some will be willing to do it for you, others will not.

Healthcare

Chile has a two tiered healthcare system, public and private. The public system is open to Chileans and is funded by a tax on everyone's paychecks. The private system is made up of private doctors and clinicas. You either need private insurance or cash/credit card or a combination of the three. You can take the money that is taxed out of your paycheck and use it to purchase an Isapre, basically a Chilean HMO. Chileans with money have Isapres and won't go to the public system. The public system is mostly used by people who don't have much money or the retired.

An Isapre costs about what a US health plan costs for a healthy person. If you're a foreigner, you can get travel insurance, but generally these max out at $10,000, so if something major happens to you, you're kind of screwed. They're designed to supplement a traditional policy. You can also look for US or European based policies that treat Chilean doctors as out of network and pay slightly lower benefits. I have a plan that pays in network for emergencies and out of network for other charges. I haven't ever had to use it, but it's a good plan if you don't want to get into the Chilean healthcare insurance system.

The private hospitals are generally really good and have standards up to a US or European top-notch hospital. The public hospitals have lower quality, longer wait times and generally are not as good. Be sure you have some sort of insurance because even in the public plan, you may end up liable for some amount of charges.

SECTION 3

Education

Chile's education system is divided into public, 45% of students, and private with 55% of students. The public schools, with the exception of a small handful of primary schools, one university (Universidad de Chile), and a few technical schools, are generally pretty poor quality. Private schools are split between true private schools and "subsidized" private schools, similar to voucher schools in the US. Anyone with means sends their kids to a true private school. Some are religious, others are simple for profit schools. Private education seems to be fairly decent, but it's expensive. The university system isn't up to US standards except for Universidad Católica, a private university, and Universidad de Chile. There are a few other universities that have good programs in different areas, but overall they aren't very good.

If you come to Chile with kids, don't expect to put them in public education if you want them to get a good education. Expect to pay $150.000-$300.000 (US$300-$600) or more per month for decent primary and high schools. Many are religious schools, although there are many non-religious traditional schools and some Montessori schools that are starting to get popular, but expect to pay. Good schools are notoriously competitive and can have waiting lists, so be sure to start your research before you come to Chile. It's not as simple as just putting them in public school like you might in the US.

There have been protests, sometimes violent, led by high school and university students who demand free, universal education and improvements to the state funded schools. There hasn't been much progress and there are still marches during the school year nearly every week. The government shut down one university, Universidad del Mar, because it was providing such terrible education and ripping off its students, all the while making large profits. Education is a huge problem in Chile for most Chileans and is one of the things holding Chile back from realizing its full potential.

Chapter 7

Safety

Chile is a very safe country, especially if you follow basic common sense. You should feel comfortable walking around during the day in every part of the city I'll cover in this book, anywhere from La Moneda up. At night, the center gets a bit dicey in places and you shouldn't walk alone until you're completely comfortable and don't have any valuables with you. I wouldn't walk around really drunk, but I guess that's just good life advice in new country! Bellavista and Bellas Artes are safer than the center, but still can be a bit dangerous if you are displaying valuables or are clearly really drunk, making yourself a target for muggers. Try not to wear expensive jewelry or earrings and don't carry your iPad or smart phone out in the open if you can avoid it. Always keep an eye on your stuff. In a country where 80% of the population makes less than a new iPhone per month, you just have to be a bit more watchful.

Providencia, Las Condes and Vitacura are generally safe at all times. I've never had a problem in any part of the city, but friends have been mugged in the center late at night after drinking or outwardly displaying valuables.

There have been isolated "snatch and grab" robberies in Providencia where thieves have stolen wallets and cell phones…you can generally avoid these by staying aware.

The biggest crime you have to worry about is getting your bag or cell phone stolen. Always be very attentive of your bag and never let it out of your site. Better yet, never let it out of your touch. Many foreigners have had their computers, bags and other documents stolen, but it's easily avoidable if you follow common sense. Don't take your phone out of your pocket and put it on a restaurant or bar table in most parts of the city. It's easy for someone to walk by and grab it…then it's gone.

If you have a backpack, never put it down unless it's wrapped around your leg or between your feet. If you go to a café or bar, don't rely on the strap connected to the chair, wrap a backpack strap around your leg and put the bag between your feet. It might be a bit uncomfortable, but it's worth keeping your bag. Thieves look for any unattended or unattached bag and steal them frequently. Be alert and you should be fine.

On the metro and the bus, take off your backpack and put it between your feet or hold it in front of you to avoid people stealing things from behind you. In the center and late at night in Bellavista and even Providencia, avoid talking for extended periods of time on your smartphone in the middle of the street. You'll likely be fine, but it's not unheard of for thieves to steal phones out of people's hands and run off. Be alert, don't act like a crazy foreigner and follow common sense and you'll be ok. Guns involved in muggings are very rare in Chile, if you are mugged it will likely be with no weapon or a small knife. If someone tries to rob you, either run away, or give up your wallet. It's not worth taking a risk.

If you have a bike, never leave it unlocked and unattended. Never leave it outside overnight or for extended periods, even if you have a lock. Always bring it into your apartment. Bikes get stolen fairly often. Be careful.

Don't let your credit or debit cards out of your sight, as thieves like to clone cards and steal from you. In Chile it can be hard to get this money back, so make sure your waiter or sales person brings the portable machine to your table and you see them swipe the card. Check ATMs for card readers before you withdraw money…if anything seems off, go to another ATM. If you use a credit or debit card issued by a US or European bank, you'll likely have the anti-fraud protection you do back home. Make sure to contact your financial institution ahead of time to double check.

To reiterate, don't leave anything in a taxi; you'll most likely never get it back. When you get out of a taxi, make sure you've left the door open so that a taxi driver can't just drive away with your stuff. Try to take your stuff out of the car before getting out and always pay the driver after you've taken your stuff out. Most taxis won't steal your stuff, but it's good protocol anywhere in the world.

Keep an eye on your purses. Pickpockets are fairly common, but if you don't display wealth, you'll be fine. I've met a few girls who have had expensive looking earrings ripped from their ears in the center, so it's good policy not to do it.

Don't ever let anyone you don't know use your cell phone, that's almost always a scam. They'll take off running and you won't see it again. If someone asks to see your id on the street with any sort of excuse, don't do it. They want you to take out your wallet and as you're taking out your id, they'll grab the whole thing and run. If the person is insistent, tell them you'd be happy to show your ID to a police office and they'll go away. I had a guy tell my friend and I and we matched the description of someone who had just put a knife to his sister's throat and he wanted to see our IDs to make sure it wasn't us. That's a clear scam. Don't fall for it.

Another scam is to ask tourists if they saw someone running with a bag/backpack, luggage etc because it was stolen. These people are scammers trying to get you to stop and let your guard down. These types are likely in touristy areas, but if you keep your guard up, nothing will happen. Be wary of scummy looking people who speak to you in English right out of the blue. That's been a precursor to theft or attempted theft many times. They prey on tourists and foreigners who don't know any better. Be aware in bus stations, just like in any country, and if someone robs you, just start yelling "ladrón", thief in Spanish. You might get your stuff back.

Chileans don't wear their seat-belts in the backseat of cars and make fun of those who do as nerdy. Don't fall into the trap of peer pressure. Wear your seatbelt. Chileans have a high incidence of car accidents compared to the US. which in my experience is based on drunk driving, poorly maintained cars and driver inattention. Wear your seatbelt. And tell Chileans they're idiots for not wearing their seatbelt in the backseat. Let's change the culture!

Be careful in the parks below Plaza Italia after dark. You'll probably be safe, but that's the only place I've ever had anyone threaten to rob me. Use common sense and be vigilant. I've never been robbed and if you look like you know where you're going and walk confidently, you'll likely be just fine.

Like other major cities, there are dangerous areas in Santiago and other parts of Chile where most of the crime is concentrated. As long as you don't go there and otherwise use common sense and be vigilant, you should be just fine. If you have problems, the Chilean emergency number equivalents to 911 are 131 for an ambulance, 132 for firefighters and 133 for police. If something happens be sure to "dejar una constancia" which is leaving a police report with the Carabineros. It will make insurance claims much easier, but won't likely get your stuff back.

Chapter 8

How Much Spanish Do I Need To Know?

Hardly anyone speaks English fluently outside of the upper class or the highly educated, maybe 5% of the country or less. Taxi drivers don't speak English, neither do bank tellers, waiters and just about anyone else you'll run into on the street. You might find a few English speaking waiters in El Golf or Lastarria, where they deal with foreigners a bunch, but anywhere else, don't count on it. Upper class Chileans are shocked when I say this because most of their friends and family speak English, but it's true. I've run into a handful of Taxi drivers in three years who speak English, whereas in Buenos Aires many taxistas do.

Although you may not be able to communicate in English, people are very friendly and will help you get around with hand signals, pointing and smiles. For example, when my Dad came to visit, a friendly 10 year old Chilean used hand signals to help him find the right spot to swipe his metro card to get on the subway. You most certainly don't need to speak Spanish to travel or even to live in Chile, but you'll get so much more out of your experience if you can at least speak a bit of Spanish and it'll be much less frustrating.

Chilean Spanish is not much like what you might have learned in high school, college or even Mexico. Chilean Spanish is the Scottish of the Spanish-speaking world. Chileans speak very fast, don't pronounce multiple letters in words and pepper their sentences with slang that other Spanish speakers don't use. They also change the ending in the *tu* form of verbs when speaking informally. For example, are you going to the movies would normally be *"vas al cine?"* but in Chilean Spanish, many times it's *"vai al cine?"*

Most Chileans don't pronounce the final Ss and Ds in many words. For example, *departamentos amoblados*, furnished apartments, is generally pronounced as *departamento amoblao*. Notice the dropped "s" from departamentos and the "d" and "s" from amoblados. Other times random S's are dropped; I lived near a street called "El Bosque" for a while, which should be pronounced "el boss-kay" but if I say it that way, most taxi drivers looks confused. If I say "el bo-kay" without the S, the taxi drivers get it

Even if you speak some Spanish, I strongly suggest taking some classes before you arrive and then an immersive class when you get here. After that, try to speak as much as you can. Everyone will tell you the best way to learn is by working in Spanish, dating a Chilean or making friends. Force yourself out of your comfort zone and you'll start to learn. It'll take a month or two, maybe more, for Chilean Spanish to slow down, but then you'll start to understand. If you already speak Spanish, check out some Chilean movies or watch old news reports to get a hang of the accent.

Check out Chapter XXX for a more in depth Chilean Spanish slang dictionary.

Chapter 9

Business Climate

lthough Chile is the most developed country in Latin America, it still has a long way to go to become a full member of the developed economy club. Santiago is the center of business, but there are plenty of opportunities in the regions, especially in mining, agriculture, aquaculture, alternative energy and tourism. The economy is controlled by a few large conglomerates, which are controlled by a few elite families. Businesses are very conservative. Chile has enjoyed high growth since the 1990s, especially in the mining, banking, agriculture and consumer products sectors. 61% of Chileans are in the workforce, 74% of men and 49% of women.

Most of these companies don't pay well in comparison to US or Europe. Companies generally don't reward longevity; many companies prefer to fire experienced workers who are earning a decent amount in favor of low paid new people, especially in sales. It's hard to get a good job unless you're well connected, highly educated or a foreigner. There's really low unemployment, currently around 6%, but most of the growth is tied to the mining sector and currently construction. If you want to know more about working, check out Chapter XXX; if you want to know about entrepreneur-ship or starting your own business check out Chapter XXX.

Santiago is the center of business, but there are plenty of opportunities in the regions, especially in mining, farming, fishing, alternative energy and tourism. Businesses are very conservative and the economy is controlled by a few large, mostly family owned, conglomerates. When you're outside of the circles of power it's incredibly hard to get something done, but when you make it inside, it's much easier. In the US, this is true as well, but in Chile it's much more pronounced. Most businesses are in the business of extracting value and arbitrage, not actually creating much new value.

In Chile, connections and networking are super important. It's what gets things done. People with power generally hold classist attitudes and are not willing to take a risk to foster entrepreneurship. People use connec-tions to get jobs, just like everywhere else in the world, but the difference is that in Chile, people are proud about using their connections to get a job. They'll happily brag that their uncle's best friend is the owner of the company and helped them get the job. In the US, people hide their insider status as much as possible.

Don't be put off if people are late to meetings. It's normal. Chileans hate to say "no." Instead they'll act very interested until it's time to pay and sign on the dotted line. You'll learn to differentiate between the "maybe" or "interested" that really means no. A "yes" can have three different mean-ings: a true yes, no, but they think it's impolite to say no, and no, please don't bother me anymore. It'll be frustrating, but you'll be able to do it if you work at it. Expect people to work long hours, but not get as much done as you might expect. Expect people to miss deadlines and expect bureaucratic delays.

There are lots of games and it's more like a battle, rather than a part-nership, especially if you are outside of the power circles. Many Chileans negotiate in a very "special" way. If they ask 100 and you counter with 80, they might say 105. The best way to deal with it is to ignore them and wait, they'll likely come back with something more reasonable.

If you want to collect payment from another company, you must have your own company. They won't pay an individual. Payment terms are generally 30-90 days after receiving invoices, but don't be surprised if it takes 120 days or if companies just ignore payment due dates. Chile is likely the best place to work in Latin America and has the best business climate, but it can still be very frustrating because of cultural differences and bureaucracy. It's really hard to open a bank account. Chilean banks ask for at least three months of income over at least $500.000 (US$1000) and permanent residence, but this is starting to change.

All of that said, if you want to start a business you can get things done here, and there are a myriad of opportunities. If you learn how the game is played and work on your networking, you can have lots of success. It's an advantage to be a foreigner because Chileans can't place you into a class structure and if you have a solid business and execute your plans, you'll have a fair chance to be successful. My advice is to find a mentor and a local partner who can help you navigate the business culture and guide you through the process.

Chilean employees are very talented, motivated and ready to work for salaries way cheaper than in the US. The minimum wage is $210.000 (US$380) per month and 80% of Chileans survive on less than $400.000 (US$800) per month. The difficulty is that they crave stability, so they'd rather work at a stable, big company with a lower salary than a "risky" startup. If you want to hire people in Chile, you'd better incorporate or pay an above market salary. The key is proving that you'll provide stability for your employees, not necessarily the highest market salary. The best way to look for programmers is to go to meetup and go to universities. You need to meet programmers in their element and convince them that you are for real, not just some fly by night entrepreneur who will leave them without a job.

For example, a friend of mine needed to hire someone for three-month contract job. He was willing to pay 3x market rate. The Chilean computer programmer who he wanted to hire accepted a full time job at market rate that guaranteed him at least 12 months of employment. Frustrating if you're a startup, but that's how many Chilean employees think.

You can either hire someone as a contractor (boleta de honrarios) or with a contract with a fixed salary. If you pay someone a salary, you're required to contribute money toward their pension plan and their healthcare. These contributions come out to about 20% of the paycheck. It is hard to fire someone, even with cause. Chile's labor laws require paying severance, the "finiquito" if you leave your job for virtually any reason. A finiquito can be up to one month's salary for each year of service at the company, plus any unused vacation time. After working for seven months, my finiquito was over a month's salary. While Chile is the most free market of any South American country, there are still barriers.

When you're outside of the circles of power it's incredibly hard to get something done, but when you make it inside, it's much easier. In the US, this is true as well, but in Chile it's much more exaggerated. In Chile, connections and networking are super important. It's what gets things done. People with power generally hold classist attitudes and are not willing to take a risk to foster entrepreneurship.

We explain this situation to entrepreneurs we meet with at Magma Partners this way: If an entrepreneur creates a solution that generates US$1M of value and they want to sell to a large business, the large business will likely not even take the meeting because they don't want to bother making changes. But if the startup is able to get to a meeting, and the company likes the solution, they'll likely demand $90% of the benefit and leave 10% for the entrepreneur, or worse.

Unless the entrepreneur is a member of the Chilean elite. Then the large business will feel "verguenza" or shame that you're taking advantage of a new company and likely be willing to agree to a more 50-50 deal. Sometimes a connected entrepreneur can even do better than that. One of the ways that we've hacked the system is by using my partner Francisco Saenz's credibility with the Chilean business elite to push for fair treatment of our entrepreneurs. We've seen it work and you can hack the system to by finding a local partner who can help you navigate the local norms and class distinctions.

I'm not saying you can't do it on your own, but it's extremely hard. One of my friends from the Pilot Round of Start-Up Chile in 2010, a German entrepreneur, found himself in a negotiation with a large Chilean retailer. The retailer wanted to do business and offered $500/month for the service. Without saying a word, he walked out of the meeting. The retailer was dumbstruck. They called back a month later and offered $1500/month. The entrepreneur walked about again, without a word. Two months later, the business called back and offered him ~$15,000/month and they closed a deal. I'm not advocating this strategy, but if you don't have a good connection, brute force negotiation is likely the only way.

Chile is one of the better places in Latin America to think about starting a business. According to the World Bank, it takes eight times less time and 90% less capital to start a business in Chile compared to the rest of Latin America. Although the market is small, only 17m people, it's stable, growing at about 5% per year in 2012. It doesn't have much entrepreneurial competition if you're interested in starting your own business. Chileans are generally conservative and would rather work in big companies, taking few risks and generating cash each month. Most people look down on entrepreneurs, although it's starting to change. In 2010 when Chileans would ask me what I did and I said I was an entrepreneur or had my own business, they'd gaze back with a puzzled look on their faces and many times would ask "so...you don't have a job?" with a complete lack of understanding. Now startups are a fashionable thing to do in some parts of society, but the vast majority would rather work in a big company.

Compared to the US, there are huge amounts of bureaucracy and paperwork, along with many laws that support incumbent players, but the system does work. You don't have to worry about bribing anyone or that the government will change the rules at the last minute when you start having success. Chile is doing everything it can to encourage business creation and entrepreneurship. They recently passed a law that allows you to create a business in one day, for free. Before it look at least 3 weeks. One of my businesses took 3 months to be fully registered. It's hard to get a bank account and you're lucky if big companies pay you within four months. Banco del Estado recently launched an entrepreneur's account that lets you get a bank account if you have a legally registered business. Asech, Chile's association of entrepreneurs, has pushed through reform bills that no longer require going to a notary to start a business and have been a great voice for entrepreneurs in Chile.

Despite its difficulties, Chile is still a good place to do business. There are so many opportunities and little to no competition. If you're willing to put up with the hassles of the system for a while and have a good idea that fixes a real problem, you can have success in Chile. The government also has programs like Startup Chile and Corfo, which support entrepreneurs financially. Further, the government is supporting accelerators and investors with public money to help foster entrepreneurship. The next few subchapters will focus on starting a business in Chile, government programs like Startup Chile and Corfo, investors and the entrepreneurial climate.

Section 1

Opportunities for Chilean Entrepreneurs

There are a multitude of opportunities in Chile for entrepreneurs to solve. From traditional businesses with good customer service, to tech startups, there's a business model that can make money to be found. After living in Chile for six years, I think the best two business models for tech starts are the ones that we invest in at Magma Partners:

1. B2B businesses that sell to large companies in Latin America that increase efficiency, sales or improve business processes.
2. Tech startups with real, money generating, business models that can have their technology teams and/or back office team in Latin America, but whose main market is the US or Europe.

Chile is not a poor country; but its wealth is very unequally distributed. This distribution means that many business models that make sense in the US don't make sense in Chile. I've seen hundreds of ecommerce and sharing economy business plans over the past six years, but both of these business models are extremely tough in chile for structural reasons. I wrote a case study on ecommerce opportunities in Chile after doing some experimentation with my friends from 2012-2015.

Start-Up Chile

Startup Chile is a government program started in 2010 that invites startups from anywhere in the world to come to Chile to start their business. It's what brought me to Chile originally. Each startup gets CLP$20,000,000 (US$40,000), free office space and a visa to be in Chile for one year. Since 2010, over 700 companies have come to Chile for the program and the goal is to change Chile's culture and diversify the economy.

Any startup can apply for Start-Up Chile, but in my mind, there are three categories of startups that would benefit most from the program.

First, companies that are either at the idea stage or have just started hacking on a prototype. They are companies that need to put their heads down and knock out a minimum viable product. To them, location doesn't matter. They benefit from Start-Up Chile for three reasons.

One, they take advantage of cheaper living costs with great quality of life. Two, if they need to hire programmers, it's cheaper and less competitive than hiring in the Bay Area or NYC. Three, they can put themselves away from distractions and come out with a great product that's ready for investors and users without having to give up any equity or take on debt.

The second type of company that would benefit are companies that have already received some funding, but are struggling to figure out their business model and need a bit of cash to get them to profitability or another round of funding. My company, Entrustet, was a perfect example of one of these startups. We'd been in business for a year and a half, launched our product, raised money and gotten a ton of press, but we still were struggling to figure out a business model that worked for us. We had money in the bank, but knew that we could extend our runway for another 6 months if we moved to Chile.

The third type of company that will benefit from startup Chile is a company that is attacking the South American market. A great example of this type of company is Intern Latin America. They are a company with founders from the UK and Colombia who place young people searching for internships in South American companies in Chile, Argentina and Colombia. They were already doing business in South America and were going to move here anyway. They got free money, connections and a great base of operations to attack South America by being in Startup Chile. They've used the Startup Chile money to build a real business dedicated to serving South America.

Companies that need to be making sales and have a defined business model and whose target is not in South America would be better served being in business centers near their clients. Making sales to customers outside of Chile is harder because of the greater distance. It makes more sense to be closer to your clients.

If you want to apply for Startup Chile, check out http://www.startupchile. org, or check out my blog, http://www.nathanlustig.com, where I've blogged extensively about the program. I also offer consulting to teams who are interested in applying. If you'd like more information, please email me, nathanlustig@gmail.com.

Since 2010, Start-Up Chile Seed has attracted over 1800 entrepreneurs to Chile. They do this with 2 application periods per year where they accept 100 companies in each round. They open the application window for 2-5 weeks and accept unlimited applications. You must fill out a short form about your project, milestones, your team and what you will bring to the Chilean entrepreneurial ecosystem. Although the video is optional, it's incredibly important. If you don't have a video, my guess is you likely won't be selected. So make a good video.

My alumni friends and I have judged applications before and many judges only look at your website, your video and short company description.

If it doesn't make sense or inspire confidence, many judges will not even bother reading the rest very closely. Judges are swamped and pressed for time. Take the time to make a good video and a high fidelity landing page. It's worth it.

Start-Up Chile uses Younoodle as their application management platform. It's not great, but it's what we have to use. I suggest writing your entire application in Google docs or Word and then copying and pasting the entire finished product into your app when you're done. I know entrepreneurs who have lost their application by saving it in Younoodle and later being unable to retrieve it. Better to be safe than sorry.

Once you finish your application, you must upload the following documents: passport, letter of recommendation, CV, etc. Once you submit your app, you can edit it until the app process closes.

Pro tip: if you don't finish your video in time, use a bit.ly or similar link that doesn't change and point it to your completed video.

Once the application process closes, it's up to the judges. Younoodle provides entrepreneurs, professors and investors as judges for the program and at least 2-3 people will review your app and give it a score on 1-5 on different areas. Younoodle ranks the applications into three categories: yes, no and maybe. The no's are thrown out immediately and then the yes' are looked at systematically and accepted on a case-by-case basis. If there are additional places, Start-Up Chile moves into the maybes and selects some of them. They aim at accept 100 companies per round. About 2000 companies have been applying for each round, so you have about a 5% acceptance rate.

After about a month of judging, winners and losers are notified by email and you have a bit of time to decide if you'd like to come to Chile. You have two arrival windows and you have to come during those times so that you can be part of orientation and get to know your fellow startups.

In my opinion, the most important parts of the application are the strength of your team, your business model and how you will contribute to Chile's entrepreneurship culture. What kind of experiences can you add to the entrepreneurial ecosystem? How can you connect your networks at home with your new Chilean networks?

Talk about your experience, your desire to give back to Chile, how you like sharing ideas and meeting other entrepreneurs. Talk about how you're going to use Chile as an incubator market and then expand internationally. Your target market shouldn't just be Chile. They are looking for global reach.

Don't be afraid to be creative in your application. Most companies that applied created standard PowerPoint videos about their business. And be sure to emphasize how you'll help support the Chilean entrepreneurial ecosystem. Don't worry if you're not chosen the first time you apply. Make your app better, continue to work and apply again. One of my friends applied and got denied, refined his idea and then got accepted in the next round.

SECTION 3

Chilean Venture Capital Overview

Chile's VC and investment community was in its infancy in 2010, when Start-Up Chile was just getting started. Supported by Corfo, part of the Chilean government, Chilean VC funds that apply for government money get up to $3 back from the government for every dollar invested. For example, if a Chilean VC makes an investment of US$1,000,000, the government will be providing up to US$750,000 of the money, with no downside risk to the fund. If the fund loses money, the government money is forgiven. If the fund makes money, they have to pay back the original $750k with interest.

There is plenty of cash around, but most VCs still are not using the same business practices as they do in the US. Since 2010, more funds have opened their doors, including my fund, Magma Partners, which bring US style investment deals to Chile. We've chosen to forgo government capital, as it allows us to be more agile, get more deals done more quickly and we think it gives us more skin in the game, which helps us be more successful.

Let's start with a quick overview of the Chilean Venture Capital ecosystem:

Private Investors

Magma Partners – We're the only fully private investment fund in Chile. We invest early stage and like to be first investors into companies. We'll do initial investments of $25-$75k and can follow on with up to $250,000 per company. We like two niches: B2B businesses in Latin America and companies that have their back office in Latin America, but whose primary market is in the US or Europe. 27 investments in 3 years. $5m fund. Presence in Chile, Colombia, Mexico, USA.

Public-Private VCs

The Chilean government, via CORFO, offers venture capital funds incentives to invest in Chile. For every $1 funds invest, CORFO can match an additional $2 or $3 with low interest debt that they forgive if you fail, but you must repay if you're successful. Here's the full fund list across all industries. These are the more startup focused funds.

Nazca/Mountain – In 2015, Nazca was acquired by Mountain Partners, a successful German/Swiss VC and company builder. They generally invest $200k-$500k in companies that can scale regionally and potentially expand to other mountain offices in Europe, Asia and Africa. Nazca has offices in Argentina, Chile, Brazil, Colombia and Mexico. Mountain has offices in multiple countries across Asia, Africa and Europe.

NXTP Labs – Early stage seed accelerator with offices across Latin America. Their standard deal is that NXTP has a $25,000 option to invest via a SAFE with a $250,000 cap that's exercisable for one year. This means that if you accept the NXTP acceleration program, you go through the program without receiving money, then, over the next year, NXTP decides if they want to invest $25k in your company. NXTP also has significant funds to do follow on in their portfolio. NXTP regional portfolio.

Chile Ventures – Biotech focused fund scheduled to launch in late 2016.

FEN Ventures – Operations in Latin America, office in Chile. Website doesn't list active investments.

Endurance Ventures – Private equity fund with a new fund launching for venture capital. One tech investment in their portfolio. At least $250k ticket sizes, likely higher.

Manutara Ventures – A new fund that's launching in 2017 with tickets of at least $200k.

Scale Capital (Ex-Inversur) – $35M fund that invests $3m checks and above. 5 investments since 2013.

Aurus – Later stage investments, usually $2m and up. Less active since 2013. Aurus has a specific fund only for mining technology as well. Aurus portfolio.

Company Investors

Wayra – Wayra Chile is part of the investment arm of Telefonica/Movistar. They invest in startups generally with $50k + $25k of services for 5-10% equity on convertible notes. Wayra can be flexible for startups with significant traction. They seem to prefer B2B companies that can be Telefonica clients or have products that they can sell to their clients. We've done two coinvestments with Wayra. and they have offices regionally in Latin America and Spain.

Government Incubators

The Chilean government, via CORFO, sponsors Chilean incubators. These incubators receive up to CLP$200m (US$310k) in grants for operations each year. The administrator needs to spend 25% of the grant from their own pocket. Incubators don't invest their own money. The award CORFO's $60m (US$90k) SSAF grants. In exchange, they (generally) receive 7% equity in the startup. CORFO receives nothing.

Each incubator has slightly different selection processes, funding stages, incubation (or lack thereof) and potential buyback clauses. You can find the list of 18 incubators on CORFO's site. These incubators have their positives and negatives. Make sure to do your due diligence before signing anything, as some have fairly entrepreneur unfriendly terms.

Equity Free Government Grants

Start-Up Chile – Start-Up Chile is the flagship program from CORFO and the Chilean government. It has financed more than 1300 Chilean and foreign startups since 2010 with its Seed program: CLP$20m pesos (US$30k) equity free grants. In 2015, Start-Up Chile added Scale, a CLP$60m pesos (US$90k) equity free follow on, and S-Factory, a CLP$10m, US$15k pre-accelerator for female entrepreneurs.

ProChile – Chilean government program that gives Chilean startups grants to expand abroad. Offices all over the world.

CORFO – You can apply for government grants from startups, to salmon to other strategic industries direct via CORFO's website.

Equity Crowdfunding

Broota – Equity crowdfunding platform for Chilean startups. Each backer buys direct equity in the company. . $3.5m invested in 16 startups since 2012. Like equity crowdfunding sites in the US, valuations here are high, in my opinion. Successful Investments.

Investment Syndicates

Founderlist.la – Founderlist is modeled after AngelList but for Latin America. They also run Emprendedores Anónimas, the largest entrepreneurial meetup group in Latin America. (I'm an investor via Magma Partners). Founderlist does a great job connecting entrepreneurs with angel investors and venture capital funds across Latin America.

Social Entrepreneurship

Socialab – Organization that helps social entrepreneurs with training and small, equity free grants.

Angel Networks

Chile Global Angels – Angel network with 20-50 active investors. 20 investments since 2010. Chile Global Angels portfolio.

Dadneo – $1.5m of investments since 2012, but seemingly slower velocity since 2013. Dadneo portfolio.

Family Offices

As of 2016, Chilean family offices have not made many startup investments so far, as most don't understand how VC is different from private equity or don't see the value in startups yet.

MAGMA PARTNERS

In 2010, there were very few private startup investors and those who were investing generally treated startups like any other private equity investment. They generally asked for controlling interests and invested at very low valuations, which were company killers. By 2012, I realized I was doing everything an investor does, besides giving money to startups and decided I wanted to start the first US style venture capital fund in Chile.

By 2013, I'd created a plan and got connected with Francisco Saenz, who heads up one of Chile's most interesting Family Offices. Along with Diego Philippi, who was part of Start-Up Chile's founding team, we started Magma Partners in December 2013. As of this writing, we're just over three years in and have become Chile's most active investor.

We originally planned to invest in 4-6 Chile based companies per year, but quickly found that demand for private capital, high quality mentorship and a bridge to the US market outstripped our modest goal.

We like to be the first investor in a startup and invest an average of $50k initially, with the capacity to follow on with $250k more. We focus on two niches:

- B2B companies that serve the Latin American market
- Startups whose tech team is based in Latin America but whose primary market is the US.

In 2016, we invested in 7 new companies, moved to new offices in Santiago and expanded our presence in Colombia and in the US. We've honed our expertise in helping Latin American startups derisk the jump to the US market and have had our first successes helping B2B companies in Latin America negotiate significant deals with legacy companies.

We also focused on building out our networks in Colombia, Mexico and the US. As more of our companies started to expand outside of Chile, it was the logical next step to live up to our promise of helping entrepreneurs with more than just money.

As we turn 3, here's some of our 2016 stats:

- ~200 new applications from 8 countries
- 7 new investments, 28 total
- 20 operating. 8 failed.
- 2014 – 13 new investments. 7 operating. 6 failed.
- 2015 – 8 new investments. 6 operating. 2 failed.
- 2016 – 7 new investments. 7 operating. 0 failed.
- First investment in Colombia
- 10 companies with US clients, 6 with US operations
- Helped 6 companies secure outside follow on funding
- 4 companies raised follow on funding in the US
- 10 profitable companies
- 49 entrepreneurs from 9 countries with 163 employees from 17 countries

The Latin America startup ecosystem is getting stronger every year. Entrepreneurs have a better understanding of how they need to compete in order to be successful. More entrepreneurs are blogging, doing events and sharing knowledge. More investors are starting to understand that they can't treat startups like private equity. And there were more acquisitions and funding of Latin American startups than ever before. The future is bright for Latin America based startups.

Note: If you're an entrepreneur whose company fits our two niches or just wants feedback on their project, please fill out our online form and we'd be happy to help!

Here's a series of essays I've written for various media outlets that will give you a great base into the Chilean VC and entrepreneurial ecosystem. This first essay dates from 2012, so you'll be able to see how things have changed.

CHILE NEEDS MORE ENTREPRENEURS TURNED INVESTORS

An article titled *Capital de riesgo: críticas y cambios que proponen los emprendedores* in Pulso [Chilean business daily] shed light onto a debate that people in the Chilean entrepreneur ecosystem are really familiar with.

Entrepreneurs Wences Caceres, Tomas Pollack and Nico Orellana talked about the state of venture capital in Chile and their experiences raising capital here and abroad. Venture Capital is a very new industry here in Chile and as its own startup.

Aurus, one of Chile's VC firms, is getting it right, but the rest are experiencing some growing pains.

Many Chilean venture capitalists are former bankers and private equity managers and don't really understand what it's like to be an entrepreneur. They invest in ideas, rather than entrepreneurs They don't understand technology very well and they try to get the most equity possible (sometimes up to 60%!), rather than work with entrepreneurs to create value.

Serious funds know that they should aim to get 10-30% of the company in the first round so that the entrepreneur stays an entrepreneur and continues to feel he controls his own destiny, rather than just an employee, slaving away for his investors. This approach kills motivation in entrepreneurs and kills returns for investors. They don't use standardized term sheets like US VCs do, making it harder to close deals and easier for venture capitalists to get better deals for themselves at the expense of entrepreneurs.

Most of the world's best investors are successful entrepreneurs turned investors. Guys like Paul Graham (ycombinator), Dave McClure (500 Startups), Mark Suster (Both Sides of the Table) and more know what its like to walk in our shoes. Chile is starting to have that. Welcu, a successful Chilean startup, has taken investment from the founders of Groupon LatAm, who sold their company and are now giving back by investing in new startups. But it's more than money. They provide mentorship, advice, connections. They tell the team when they're wrong and push them to succeed.

Chile need more investors who understand that they are partners with entrepreneurs. And we know that will come as more Chilean entrepreneurs are successful. And we need entrepreneurs, journalists and companies to speak out when they believe investors are behaving badly. That's the only way things get better.

The future is very bright for Chilean entrepreneurs and we believe that as the sector matures, new funds started by successful entrepreneurs and those who understand entrepreneurship will begin to emerge. More competition will force the current funds to change or miss out on the best deals.

ARNON KOHAVI AND THE CHILEAN INVESTMENT ECOSYSTEM

Arnon Kohavi is an Israeli entrepreneur who made a big money in Silicon Valley. He became an investor and came to Chile in 2010 with the intention of starting up a Series A fund. He left after six months and wrote a scathing article about Chile's VCs, the rich and the investment community.

His post on The Next Web titled Why this investor abandoned setting up a startup fund in Chile after just 6 months has provoked heated reaction inside and outside Chile.

I've summarized Kohavi's main points about Chile and the entrepreneur ecosystem (read the entire interview) and tried to respond to each one.

"Chile is less dynamic than Asia because it is controlled by a handful of rich families who don't care about the young or the poor. They give money to support entrepreneurship, but it's only in Spanish and they do it to stroke their ego. Conservative organizations like Opus Dei and a bigoted older generation don't encourage social ascension. Chile's main problem is mental isolation, not just geographic and Chilean startups have to move abroad to be successful. The investors are private equity guys who don't know entrepreneurship or entrepreneurs. In 10 years and with education, Chile can be dynamic, but it's not ready yet. That's why I'm going to Singapore." – Arnon Kohavi

So is Kohavi right? For him, leaving in 2010 makes perfect sense because he wants to make money NOW and I'm not sure Chile actually needed a real Series A fund. In 2017, Chile has more Series A funds, but none are active. I believe there are really only 2-3 tech startups per year that can take a $1-$2m check and return capital to investors. Chile still needs more mentoring and smaller infusions of capital on the angel/micro angel scale, which is exactly what we decided to do with Magma Partners in 2013. Kohavi's business model was not correct for the time in Chile and would most likely fail in 2017 if he tried. I think if he experimented with business models, he could have made a name for himself and his fund, but instead he chose to go to Singapore. Nothing wrong with that at all. And it left a space in the market for my partners and I to start Magma Partners.

Next, he hits a wide range of issues affecting Chilean culture and the entrepreneur ecosystem and its potential for growth. Has he been fair to Chile? Lets take a closer look based on what I've seen over the past two years.

I believe that there are huge opportunities for home grown and foreign entrepreneurs in Chile and Latin America. They are just harder to execute. Chileans are smart, talented and hard working and there are some great Chilean entrepreneurs. I don't see Kohavi's article as an attack on them. In fact, I respect Chilean entrepreneurs even more because they are able to succeed in a tough environment. Entrepreneurship is hard enough in Silicon Valley. Adding in Chilean cultural barriers, small market, Chilean "chaqueteo" or tearing down successes, and a developing ecosystem adds many additional roadblocks. It's harder to be an entrepreneur in Chile than in the US.

Kohavi is right, Chile is a very conservative country controlled by a few powerful families, supported by a small, wealthy upper class. Many of these powerful families have natural resources connections. Chile is very class stratified and Kohavi is right that class ascension is not encouraged. It's not quite overtly discouraged, but it's extremely common to hear "what high school did you attend, what's your last name, are you related to so and so" in social conversations and even business meetings. People know their place and the classes really don't mix. In the US we have the American Dream , which states that if you get a good education and work hard, you can move up in society.

Whether the American Dream is actually true anymore or is now just a myth is very debatable, but upward mobility is instilled in us from the time we are 5 years old.

Like Sarah Lacy says, Chile's wealthy are no different from old monied elite in the US, Europe, or anywhere else in the world. Most elites like their power, their money and their lives and try to stay where they are and amass more land, money and power. It's normal. But Chile is unique because the elite group is small enough that innovation can be stifled. For example, I have a friend who wanted to streamline a paper heavy process for a few large companies. These companies could pass on their savings to consumers or earn more profit.

He got the right meetings through business associations and government contacts, but when he went to the sales meeting, the big wigs who organized the meeting trashed my friend's idea in front of his potential client. A few months later, my friend found out that the big wig was good friends with the guy who currently made a bunch of money managing the paperwork. My friend's solution would speed up commerce, save consumers money and time, but at the detriment of this guys friend. This behavior is normal in all countries, but Chile is small enough that it can kill startups right in the beginning. You don't need the elites to buy into entrepreneurship, but it sure helps.

Chilean culture punishes failure and taking chances. As the founder of a startup, people look at you like you're unemployed, bouncing around with no direction in your life. Companies are very conservative and there's lots of red tape, paperwork and bureaucracy. There's also a very Chilean behavior, the "soft no", where companies won't say no directly and they'll explore a deal for months on end with no desire to actually do anything. I've also noticed that many Chileans are stubborn and very very unwilling to admit that they are wrong, as losing face/honor is more looked down on than in the US or Europe. When working for startups or trying to make sales to large companies, this attitude is very hard to overcome.

People also are very open about nepotism. In the States, one of my good friends got a job because his father was friends with the CEO of the company. He does everything he can to hide that fact and works even harder to prove that he belongs. In Chile, I see many people getting jobs because of connections, just like in the US, but in Chile people are proud that they've gotten the job that way. It's almost like a badge of honor. That's not good for a merit based startup ecosystem.

I've noticed a huge difference in attitude between Chileans who have lived and worked in the US, Europe or Australia compared with Chileans who have never been abroad for significant amounts of time. Most who have lived abroad realize that being stubborn and refusing to admit they are wrong will not get them anywhere.

Kohavi was right on about most Chilean investors in 2010. I spoke to just about every Chilean VC and angel network with my Start-Up Chile start and the vast majority were bankers and private equity guys who knew nothing about startups. They were investing in ideas, not entrepreneurs. They tried to get the most equity possible (sometimes up to 60%!) and looked at it like a zero sum game, not as a partnership. Industry standard is 20-35%. This approach kills motivation in entrepreneurs and kills returns for investors. But this it's normal for a growing ecosystem, all of the VCs are learning on the fly. In 2017, it's better, but there still need to be more entrepreneurs turned investors, as many in the VC industry have a money management or traditional business background.

So where do we go from here? Chile has smart entrepreneurs, talented developers, great potential employees and has seen some successes (Needish, Zappedy, Welcu, Plataforma Arquitectura and others), but what makes life easier for entrepreneurs and really develops the Chilean startup ecosystem? It's not a bad thing that entrepreneurs have to leave Chile to succeed. That's how it is in most places not named New York or San Francisco. The key is to create the development ecosystem so that companies can hire good talent and make entrepreneurship a viable model for a higher percentage of people so that the ecosystem grows over time.

I would expand government programs to take Chilean entrepreneurs to foreign countries, to place smart, promising Chileans in top internships and jobs in the US, Europe and Australia. I would select 300+ young Chileans every year and give them grants to encourage them to go abroad. I believe that it's not good enough to bring foreign entrepreneurs to Chile and give some Chileans money from Corfo. It's a start, but only part of the solution. Chile needs to develop its intellectual capital and I think the best way to do it is to encourage Chileans to work abroad and then return home to share their experiences.

Israel's startup scene took off after ICQ was acquired for a ton of money. Same thing happened in Madison after Jellyfish. It showed everyone that they could start a startup and that it was a real career. Chile needs a similar success and will probably have one in by 2017-2018. Culture will not change without success cases that show that entrepreneurship is a viable path. It will be even better if the huge success comes from someone who's already tried another startup and it did not succeed or comes from outside of the "elite" bubble.

Overall, I think Chile is one of the most interesting places to start a business. It has smart people, an involved government, lots of problems that need solving. There are cultural issues that are holding many entre-preneurs back. Some of these challenges are normal in a growing startup ecosystem, while others are Chile specific. I think Kohavi was naive about what to expect in Chile and I don't read his interview as a knock on Chilean entrepreneurs. I still see huge potential in Chile and an ecosystem that's made huge progress in the year since I arrived in 2010. This progress is accelerating because of a virtuous cycle created Start-Up Chile, investors, entrepreneurs and organizations that support entrepreneurs. There's still a long way to go, but future is bright.

CHILE NEEDS MORE SUCCESSFUL ENTREPRENEURS TURNED VCS, PART 2

Note: I wrote this essay on my blog in 2012, before starting Magma Partners. Much of what I wrote still holds true and is part of the problem we're trying to solve with Magma Partners. We hope to help jumpstart the virtuous cycle I talked about in the last section by helping entrepreneurs become success-ful so that they can be Chile's version of Dave McClure or Paul Graham.

I fully believe that Chile's VC industry is in its infancy, but that Chile doesn't need more Series A funds. It needs someone like Dave McClure or Paul Graham. An article in Pulso, a Chilean business daily, titled Venture Capital: Critiques and changes proposed by entrepreneurs (Spanish), has brought startup funding mainstream in Chile. As far as I know, this article, written in May 2012 by Javiera Quiroga, is the first one in a major news-paper talking about the problems occurring in Chilean venture capital. In summary, the article interviewed three successful entrepreneurs, Chileans Tomas Pollak and Nicolas Orellana and Argentinean Wences Caseres, who shared their experiences with venture capital in Chile. To summarize:

Chilean entrepreneurs said that the vast majority of Chilean venture capital funds are not entrepreneur friendly. They don't use standardized term sheets, they try to take as much equity as possible (60%+), turning entrepreneurs into slaves, instead of partnering with entrepreneurs. They are mostly former bankers or private equity without technology experi-ence. The vast majority just give money and don't provide much else. The only way to fix the problem is for time to pass and the industry to mature.

The funds responded that there's plenty of money around and that entrepreneurs are getting funded at a high rate.

I agree with the vast majority of what the entrepreneurs say in the article. I had contact with many of Chile's investors either directly when we were looking to raise money with Entrustet and indirectly via speaking with Chilean and foreign entrepreneurs. Some people believe that the solution is more money in the Chilean investor community. If only there were more investors, they say, entrepreneurship would flourish. This mentality is still prevalent in 2017 and it's very frustrating that this myth keeps getting perpetuated.

I don't agree. More money can't hurt, but there is plenty of investor money in Chile. Startups with world-class founders who execute and deliver what they promise get money, whether it's from Chile, the US, Brazil or other countries if they attack the right markets and have built something that people want..

The problem is that more Chilean startups fail than they should. Chile has a very educated, passionate and hard working base of potential entrepreneurs who lack experience, connections and the know how to run startups. A small percentage of Chile's potential entrepreneurs are actually reaching the goals that they are capable of.

They don't fail because of a lack of money. They fail because many inexperienced entrepreneurs without networks make correctable mistakes that sink their companies. Chile doesn't need more VC. It needs smart money. It needs mentorship that comes with a check.

Chile needs mentor/investors who have successfully run startups. People who knows what lean startups are. How startups work in the US, but also understand Chilean culture. Best practices for funding. Someone to be a sounding board and tell startups when they are doing things wrong and give advice on how to make it better. Someone credible to call bullshit on poor planning and excuses. Someone to demand more and help create the roadmap to success.

Chile needs entrepreneurs turned investors who can mentor startups and give them the money they need to get a viable product that can bridge the gap to a Series A and steer them to good VC funds. This will force Chilean VCs to improve, like their Brazilian counterparts Monahees Capital, who use Silicon Valley standards in Brazil.

Two early examples are Oskar Hjertonsson and Daniel Undurraga, the founders of Needish and Clandescuento, which were later acquired by Groupon. After the acquisition, Oskar and Daniel were in charge of Groupon

LatAm's successful expansion across South America and are now investing in startups. But they're not just throwing cash at startups. They're using their expertise to mentor startups and push potential entrepreneurs to start their companies. David Basulto and David Assael, the founders of world class architecture website Arch Daily both mentor and angel invest in startups.

For example, after Nicolas Orellana organized the first Webprededor, Latin America's most important tech and entrepreneurship conference, Oskar and Daniel told Nicolas that they would fund him if he developed his event management tool and started selling it to other companies. Nicolas founded Welcu shortly thereafter. Although Nico's the type of entrepreneur who would find a way to succeed no matter what, they've been advisers and additional investors.

Welcu's now been funded by 500 Startups and has built a profitable tech startup that continues to grow in 2017. Welcu is an example of how successful entrepreneurs funded a new startup and continue to share their know how. There are other similar success stories in Chile, especially from ex-Groupon Chile employees, like Daniela Lorca, Desiree Grinspun and Pablo Viojo who started BabyTuto, one of the fastest growing ecommerce companies in Latin America. Chile needs more and it should be an organized effort.

Weonomics: Translating a Chilean's Response to A Business Proposition

Stated Answer	Real Answer	Reason	Result	Frequency
Yes	Yes	They want to do business with you	Business Deal	Rare!
Yes	No	They don't want to do business with you but believe it's rude to say no	Two months wasted meetings, emails and effort	Frequent
Yes	No	They said yes to get you to stop bothering them and hopefully go away	Two months wasted meetings, emails and effort	Moderate, Frequent in customer service
No	No	They don't want to do business with you	Move on to next deal	Rare!
No	Yes	It's possible, but they don't want to do the extra work	With follow up and pressure, you'll get the deal done	Frequent, mostly in customer service

Weonomics

I talked about how Chilean have trouble saying no. And how they can be passive aggressive. One of my most trafficked blog posts talks about this phenomenon that Skinner Layne, an entrepreneur friend of mine, coined: Weonomics.

Weonomics. Noun. The study of peculiar Chilean economic behavior in business dealings.

There are some clear cultural difference between doing business in the US and in Chile. I've taken to calling it Weonomics. (Gringo readers, weon is the ubiquitous Chilean word meaning anything from dude to asshole.) Clearly not all Chileans subscribe to the principles of Weonomics, but I run into enough people who have MBAs in Weonomics that I felt I had to write about it. I have a feeling you will find yourself in one of these situations after being in Chile at least a month.

Negotiation

A typical US negotiation:
- Seller asking price $45,000
- My offer price: $37,000
- Seller counteroffer: $43,000
- My counteroffer: $39,000
- Final price: $41,000

Pretty simple, right? A sales price, a counter offer and meet somewhere in the middle. You might think negotiation would work similarly in any part of the world, but not with many Chileans.

Weonomics:
- Seller asking price $45,000
- My offer price: $37,000
- Seller counteroffer: $48,000
- My counteroffer: See ya!

Seriously? Who in their right mind thinks they'll close a deal counter offering by RAISING their initial price? But this is a principal tenant of Weonomics. The worst case I've seen was when a friend was trying to purchase a house. The opening price was $140,000. My friend bid $120,000. The counter offer? $210,000. Weonomics at its finest.

Lowball/HighBall

Someone's first offer is rarely close to a real offer. It's almost always a borderline insultingly lowball offer, or a pie in the sky number that only an idiot would pay. A friend closed a deal with a major Chilean company that pays him $15,000 per month. Their first offer? $500 per month. Many Chilean real estate prices are listed above market value in hopes that someone will come along and just buy it. You'll rarely find a business deal that's priced to get a deal done quickly.

Meeting Cancellations and No Shows

I've been stood up more in the past six months that I ever have been in my entire life combined. I had a string of five meetings on a random Monday and Tuesday that all cancelled less than 30 minutes before the meeting was supposed to start. Two didn't show up, not bothering to even tell me. One of the no shows told me it was my fault because "maybe I didn't understand Spanish fully." The only problem? She'd emailed me the day before explicitly setting the meeting. It was impossible to mistake. That's Weonomics.

No/Yes

You rarely ever hear a true yes or no in Chilean business. Each answer can mean multiple things. See chart:

One time I ordered sushi for delivery on a national holiday. The person who answered the phone told me I shouldn't order because it would be an hour and a half wait for my food. I thought about it, but put the order in anyway and made myself a small snack to tide myself over. 20 minutes later, my sushi arrived, just as I was finishing my snack. Her no, it'll take too long, was simply trying to get out of more work. Weonomics at work.

Pay attention in your first few months in Chile and you'll notice these behaviors. There's nothing you can do to change them, so it's best to be aware of Weonomcis so that when they strike, you don't take it personally.

Weonomics: Translating a Chilean's Response to A Business Proposition

Stated Answer	Real Answer	Reason	Result	Frequency
Yes	Yes	They want to do business with you	Business Deal	Rare!
Yes	No	They don't want to do business with you but believe it's rude to say no	Two months wasted meetings, emails and effort	Frequent
Yes	No	They said yes to get you to stop bothering them and hopefully go away	Two months wasted meetings, emails and effort	Moderate, Frequent in customer service
No	No	They don't want to do business with you	Move on to next deal	Rare!
No	Yes	It's possible, but they don't want to do the extra work	With follow up and pressure, you'll get the deal done	Frequent, mostly in customer service

How To Recruit and Retain Latin American Talent

One of a founder's most important duties is identifying and recruiting top talent. Finding and convincing the best people to work for your startup can be the difference between success and failure. There are hundreds of great resources on how to find great talent in the US, but Latin America is very different. US strategies don't usually work in Latin America.

Recruiting for startups in the US is difficult because the market is extremely competitive and well developed. But it can be easier because many people want to work at a startup because "startups are cool." Sometimes startups even pay well.

Many US workers choose a mission driven company that aims to change the world, or a company that offers workers the opportunity to work on interesting problems, rather than the company that pays the most or has the highest brand recognition. Additionally, structural advantages like recruiters and well developed stock options plans showcase startup opportunities and push more people to take a risk with a startup. In Latin America, it's different. It can be difficult to recruit for startups, but not because of competition from other startups.

Difficulties of Identifying Talent and Recruiting Employees in Latin America

1. Startups Aren't Cool Yet

In the US, working for a startup is cool. In Latin America, it's cool to work for an old, conservative business. Your parents, your significant other and your friends will likely be more impressed that you have a middle management job at a stodgy retailer than if you earn the same money at a startup nobody's heard of. I once told someone I "worked at a startup" and they were befuddled, asked where I worked again, and then gave me a look of pity, as if I were a jobless bum.

2. Latin Americans are generally conservative

In addition to wanting to work for conservative companies, most people would rather work for a big company because they perceive it as more secure than working for a startup. Latin America is currently going through the job losses that the US experienced in the financial crisis, and still believe mechanization isn't killing jobs, so people still don't view traditional jobs as risky.

3. Employees don't value stock options

Stock options are a new idea for most Lain American workers and, in many cases, an alien concept. Most people generally think employers are trying to screw them by offering less money, but equity in the company. They can't understand why a founder would want to give away equity to a lowly worker!

In addition, there haven't been many examples of successful employees making big money from working at a startup because there haven't been many successful startups in Latin America yet. The perceived (and maybe real) value is low, so founders lose another tool from their tool kit.

4. Top university graduates expect high salaries (for their countries)

If a Latin American went to one of the top 2-3 universities in their country, they expect a top salary that's likely out of reach for a local startup and may even be expensive for a US startup in a non engineering role.

5. Unwillingness to move

In the US, if you're a young single person and you get recruited to a top startup in California and you live in Wisconsin, chances are you'll think long and hard about going. The US has a much stronger culture of moving for jobs. In Latin America, family usually comes first, second and third, so it can be hard to get top candidates to move.

6. Risk taking is viewed as dangerous

Finding risk takers can be difficult. Most Latin Americans are generally conservative because they've been trained to optimize for keeping their heads down and not getting fired. That's antithetical to a startup, where founders push their team to take risks, fail fast and fail small, so they can avoid a big failure and be successful faster.

7. Intense work ethic is harder to find

Many people like their 15+ public holidays and 3 weeks of vacation and have a 9-6, with an hour lunch, mentality. If something needs doing outside those hours, they're not working. That's fine and there's no problem with people optimizing for free time, but a startup needs people who are willing to be a bit more flexible and are generally optimizing for other things.

8. Universities train for big businesses

This is true in the US too, but its even more of a problem in Latin America. Most workers were trained to work in a big business and lack the skill set for startups

9. People are skeptical of companies that treat them well

Many large companies rule by fear and require constant employee face time with little visible benefit. It can be strange for a worker to find a company that treats them well. I've seen well known large companies that have a standard practice of bringing everyone into a conference room once per quarter, pointing to a worker and firing them in front of everyone, with no prior warning. It's just to keep them in line.

10. Workers value contracts

In the US, you can hire a new worker as an independent contractor. In many Latin American countries, people need and want government social benefits for things like renting an apartment or getting a loan for a house, so doing the contractor route can be more difficult. Many people would rather work for an established company on a contract rather than make 3-4x as a contractor.

11. Classism and racism can make finding top candidates difficult

Many local companies and recruiters reject top talent based on classism and racism, which makes some good candidates self select out of applying.

Strategies to attract Latin American talent for your startup

Make no mistake, there are incredibly talented people in Latin America who would love to work for a startup and would be great cultural fits. Here's the strategies I've seen successful funds and startups use to recruit the best people in Latin America.

1. Show me the money!

If you're a funded startup or a US based startup…show them the money! Hire at or above market salary, use local contracts and you can likely buy yourself a good team. Chile has the highest average wages in Latin America and you only need to earn $1400 to be in the top 5% of wage earners. Other countries are even lower. If you pay an employee US$2000/month, or even US$3000/month, you'll be able to pick top talent. But this top talent that's clearly motivated by money isn't ideal, as they'll be likely to jump ship at the first higher offer.

2. Lower an employee's (perceived or real) risk

Four top funds in Latin America, including Magma Partners, guarantee great people jobs in other portfolio companies if the startup they work for goes bust or it just doesn't work out at the company they joined. We give top workers piece of mind so that they can "take a risk" by working at a startup, knowing they won't miss a paycheck.

3. Don't be like the locals: classism

Latin American countries have varying degrees of classism, which precludes some of the best people from top jobs in traditional companies. Or precludes them from advancement above lower level jobs.

50% of Chileans earn minimum wage. 90% earn less than $1400/month. Hire the best people, give them paths to advancement and you'll find an enormous untapped pool of great employees. Bonus: if you treat them well, they're more likely to be loyal since you gave them an opportunity.

4. Don't be like the locals: university degrees

Most large Latin American companies won't even look at a person's resume if they didn't complete university. Or just as bad, didn't go to one of the top 2-3 universities in their country. No degree/lower tier university=low wage work for the rest of your life.

Some of our best employees didn't finish university, either because they ran out of money, had to start working to help their families or weren't prepared to succeed in university when they were 18-20 years old. But they're brilliant and hard working. Give them an opportunity and you'll likely have a loyal, hard working employee who is just as qualified, if not more so, than someone who did finish university.

5. Don't be like the locals: company culture

Most Latin American companies value copious in office face time, rigid rules, punish failure harshly, require employees to punch the clock.... literally. Many rule by fear and don't offer opportunities for advancement.

Show that you value productivity, allow flexibility, allow space for small failures and attract great employees.

6. Give talented people something fun to work on

Like the US, many big companies in Latin America are extremely conservative. A programmer can work on maintaining old code from the early 2000s, or they can come work on the cutting edge, learning something new every day. Show you offer these opportunities.

7. Train and teach your employees

Many Latin American large companies don't push personal growth and employees can stagnate, doing the same thing over and over. Emphasize that you train your employees and teach them the newest tricks of the trade.

8. Culture of promoting from within

Most large Latin American companies don't promote from within. If you start in an entry-level position, you'll maybe get a promotion or two, but you're not going to be able to advance very far. Show that you're different.

9. Don't be like the locals: corporate culture fit

In Latin America, like the US, "can I have a beer with that person" is one of the bigger, yet unspoken, hiring criteria. In Latin America, so many smart, dedicated, people get passed over if they don't fit the prevailing culture. I think this sentiment is even stronger than it is in the US.

10. Hire women

Latin American companies can be infused with machismo. Promote a more even culture and hire smart, dedicated women and you'll be successful.

11. Interview for culture and test

More people in Latin America prefer a more laid back lifestyle than people in 2017 USA. And that's fine. But it's better to be sure that the person will fit a startup culture ahead of time, rather than just being a really smart person who can pass an interview. I always do a one to three month test with all new startup employees to make sure that they can do the job and that they are up for working in a startup.

12. Local job boards + referrals

The best place to find locals are on local job boards. International boards don't work well and you have lots of competition. Find the two biggest local job portals and post there. Join expat groups on Facebook and post there as well. Overqualified expats who either don't speak the language well enough, don't have a university degree that local companies recognize, or don't have the required paperwork make amazing employees.

In Chile, try Chiletrabajos.cl, Computrabajo and others for good tech talent.

13. Involve C level or founders in the recruiting process

People love to work with passionate teams who love what they're doing. In Latin America, most companies push hiring onto HR managers. You can be different by involving top level people in your startups.

Section 6
Punishing Failure

Chile's culture punishes failure and risk taking. Part of Startup Chile's goal is to help change the culture. Here's an essay I wrote on my blog about punishing failure:

Ever since we've gotten to Santiago, we've heard from all sorts of people about Chile's penchant for punishing failure. I recently met a twenty-six year old Chilean who graduated from one of the top universities in Chile with a degree in engineering. He spoke great English and wanted to start a business. He even had a good idea. I asked him why he hadn't started his business yet and he told me that he had a good job at a consulting firm and that he couldn't risk failure because he would never be able to get another good job if his business failed, even if it failed because of factors outside of his control.

He told me his plan: go to the US to get his MBA and then come back to Chile to start his business. He said that if he failed, he would still be able to get a job because he would be so over qualified, with better qualifications than his would be boss, that they'd have to hire him.

So, in order for this 26 year old to feel comfortable starting a business, he had to graduate from the best university in Chile, work at a top consulting firm, learn English, get an MBA from a top US university. Only then could he feel comfortable starting a business. He told me that if he started a business and failed, a potential employer would rather have a 22 year old recent grad with no experience, instead of his work and entrepreneurial experience. Talk about entrepreneurial overhead!

In the US, companies would love to hire someone who tried to start their own business out of college, even if they failed. They would call it "real world experience" and employers would like that the potential hire was a "go getter." I'm confident that if I decide I want to get a job instead of doing startups, I could. Here, it's the opposite. Most people believe that if a business fails, it's because the owner was either corrupt, stupid or both. People shun failures.

It's not exactly the best environment for creating new businesses or innovation. Many Chileans have good ideas, but they don't believe it's worth taking the risk to start a business. I also learned that making a ton of money is sort of looked down upon here. Multiple people have told me that during Chilean President Sebastián Piñera's first presidential campaign in 2010, he had to fight off attacks from the opposition that he was TOO successful. Not that he was corrupt, but that he was too successful. Now, during his run for his second term in 2017, his opponents can attack him for both being too successful and potentially corrupt!

It's a very difficult cultural difference for people who want to start businesses, but it's an opportunity for Chileans who are willing to take risks and shun cultural pressures to make money and be extremely successful. There are so many opportunities to create amazing businesses in Chile that people who can break free from the cultural pressures will create amazing businesses. That's part of the reason we are here: Start-Up Chile was created to show Chileans that starting a business is an option, failure is ok and that Chile is a great place to start a business. Seven years into the experiment, it's clearly working. There are more venture capital funds than ever to help ambitious Chilean and foreign entrepreneurs succeed.

Section 7

Case Study: Ecommerce Opportunities in Chile

In late 2012, I met up with two ex Start-Up Chile friends over beers. Like most beery conversations between entrepreneurs, the conversation devolved into new business ideas. All three of us had seen ecommerce's steady growth in Chile and were certain that it would continue to grow toward levels seen in other developed markets. After a few more beers, one of us said, "Why don't we just start a small ecommerce business, it's the best way to learn about the market and see where the real opportunities are."

That conversation led to more conversations and we got serious about launching a small ecommerce business to really get a handle on the market. But what product should we sell? And how would we validate the market to know if the product we wanted to sell made sense? And how would we do it without spending huge amounts of money?

I'm writing this post to shed light into our thought process and to show how we validated our ecommerce business without spending a single dime (peso in this case) for two reasons:

1. To give an overview of Chilean (and Latin American) ecommerce opportunities

2.   To help other entrepreneurs think about how they can validate their own ideas without spending months and thousands of dollars buying inventory, developing software and wasting time on unimportant things.

By now, almost all entrepre neurs know about lean startup methodology and try to use it, but the how remains mysterious to a high percentage of entrepreneurs. I hope this post is useful.

Step 1. Research

We first wanted to see if countries adopt ecommerce in a predictable manner. We knew that ecommerce in Chile was growing at 30% per year, but the vast majority of people hadn't ever bought anything online. We found a Forrester report that showed the phases of ecommerce adoption. It corroborated our hypothesis that new markets tended to follow similar paths:

We firmly believed that Chile was nearing the end of phase 2, and the early adopters were already moving into phase three. Chile is young and social, people are comfortable online. LAN airline ticket offices and travel agents were going out of business because of online purchases. We saw early successes like Buscalibre and Clandescuento (acquired by Groupon) and large retailers were starting to sell online. One of our best friends, Tiago Matos, is the founder of Jumpseller, a Shopify of Latin America, and we saw his business taking off. It was clear to us that we were on the cusp of phase three and we decided to go after it.

Step 2. What should we sell? A product? Or pickaxes to the miners?

We made a map of the industry in Latin America and looked at the businesses that make money in ecommerce in the US. By late 2012, we saw seven opportunities in the ecommerce market in Latin America:

1.   Amazon clone (high volume, low margin)
2.   Niche products with amazing stories and customer service (Dollar Shave Club)
3.   Create your own brand (Warby Parker)
4.   Shopify – Sell the pickaxes to the miners and create the infrastructure

5. Payment systems
6. Logistics and delivery (drop-shipping)
7. Get the exclusive representation of a foreign brand (medium margin business, low competition)

We quickly discarded doing an Amazon clone because we believed that the Amazon of Latin America will likely be Amazon or potentially Linio, from Rocket Internet, which had recently launched. We also saw Buscalibre potentially struggling and discarded that idea.

We discarded doing a Shopify clone because our friend Tiago Matos was already working on Jumpseller and having some success. We looked at payments, but although a massive problem, we didn't think we could solve it. We decided that it was likely that someone like Stripe, Braintre, Paypal or Venmo would use VC funding from the US to attack the Latin American market or a Chilean with political connections would beat us out. We looked at selling a commodity product with an amazing story, but decided that if you have a commodity product, in the medium term, your margin will go to zero.

That left us with three options:

1. Getting the exclusive distribution rights to a product that didn't exist in Chile
2. Creating our own product from scratch Warby Parker style
3. Starting with a commodity product, knowing that our margin would eventually go to zero, with the goal of adding an exclusive representation or our own product after we got clients.

We chose option three for two reasons:

1. Creating our own brand was too expensive and time consuming
2. Introduce a new brand that people didn't trust into the equation would be difficult because the vast majority of our potential clients would be buying online for the first time.

Step 3. *What product should we sell?*

We made a list of 50+ products that we were interested in selling including:

1. Diapers
2. Condoms

3. Brand Name Sunglasses
4. Birth Control Pills/tampons
5. White label Sunglasses
6. Cosmetics
7. Pet Supplies
8. Eyeglasses
9. Men's personal grooming items
10. Disposable shavers
11. Perfume
12. Women's Shoes
13. Jewelry/Accessories
14. Custom Tshirts
15. Bikes
16. Purses/Wallets
17. Wine, Beer
18. Tea and Coffee
19. Electronics Accessories (iPhone cases etc)
20. Headphones
21. Watches
22. Baby stuff
23. Women's underwear
24. Artwork
25. Vitamins
26. Soccer jerseys
27. Kids Toys
28. Home Furniture and Accessories
29. Office Furniture
30. Custom Shirts
31. Backpacks

We created a list of criteria to find the perfect product for us to start with. Our criteria was:

1. Easy to ship

Shipping in Latin America was (still is) expensive and unreliable for larger products. We needed a small, lightweight product. That quickly eliminated products like furniture, diapers, pet supplies, beer and wine.

2. High margins

We wanted to be in a high margin business, which eliminated all the low margin businesses.

3. Few Returns

Since shipping is a big problem we wanted a product with as few returns as possible.

4. Repeat orders

If we had to struggle to get our first client, and many of our clients would be buying online for the first time, we wanted them to be able to buy again. That knocked sunglasses, bikes, watches, backpacks and artwork off the list.

5. Try before you buy?

Chileans didn't trust ecommerce, so we wanted a product that you didn't have to try before you bought, which knocked a significant amount of products off the list.

6. Average cart size

We wanted an average cart size of around $30, which would allow us to give free shipping, but still allow people to buy online without taking too much risk that their expensive purchase wouldn't arrive.

7. Average item price

We wanted a lowish average price of around $5 so that the buyer would buy multiple items to get to our average cart size, and so that people could buy one cheap item to make their first ecommerce transaction low risk.

8. Market penetration

We wanted a product that was popular, but that you couldn't find on every corner.

9. Current available selection in Chile

We wanted there to be few choices in the market, so that our product was a commodity

10. Easy access to supply?

Was it easy for us to buy the product to resell? Was it available in Chile? Or did we have to import it?

11. Access to supply outside of major cities

Did people outside of major cities have a problem finding the product?

12. Poor customer buying experience and customer service after sale

Could an online experience be a better than the current offline experience? How was the post sale experience?

13. Potential competition

What did the competition in Latin America look like?

14. Press potential

Could we get into the press with this product easily?

15. Success in the US?

Was it one of the first products that was successful in the early days of the US ecommerce?

16. Do we like it/will it be fun?

One of the most important criteria. It doesn't make sense to work on something you don't like, unless you have to.

We scored all the products and quickly found that there was one product that was clearly better than the rest. It was small, lightweight, easy to ship, didn't need to be tried on, had zero returns, cost about $3 per product, but could have an average cart size of around $30. It was also a terrible customer experience to buy offline for cultural reasons, had decent margins. We had a contact in the distributor who would help us buy our initial stock quickly and easily. What was the product? After our research, we'd decided to sell condoms online.

Since Chile is a very Catholic country where sex education is almost nonexistent, we knew there wouldn't be much competition and it would be fairly easy to get press. We were also motivated to try to help solve a social problem by providing an online Sex Ed resource where scared, young people could learn about one of the most important decisions in their lives. And most of all, it would be interesting and fun.

Step 4. Validating without spending any time or money

Now that we'd chosen condoms based on our research, it was time to validate that people would actually buy them online without us spending thousands of dollars on a website and initial stock. We mapped out a plan and started to execute.

First, we looked on Mercado Libre (Latin America's Ebay) to see if people were selling condoms online. We quickly found that they were and googled to see if there were any other stores selling condoms online. There weren't, so we decided to create our own Mercado Libre listings to see if we could get any buyers. We received numerous messages from potential buyers, but we always told them we were sold out, as we didn't have any condoms to sell them. We'd found that there was a market.

Next, we put up new ads on Mercado Libre and actually made sales. When someone said they wanted to make a purchase, we walked to our local pharmacy, purchased the products and then met the buyer, usually in one of Santiago's metro stations, to make the exchange. At this point, we didn't allow online payment or shipping for two reasons:

1. We wanted to make the barrier to purchase as low as possible
2. We wanted to meet our clients to learn more about them.

We found that most of our clients were young, ignorant, uneducated, scared 15–21 year olds who were clearly going to have sex, many for the first time, and weren't comfortable buying at the pharmacy.

After about a week and ~5 purchases, we allowed people to pay online with a free instant bank transfer to validate that people would pay online. They did. After another week, we added free shipping and the orders kept coming in. We kept filling them by walking to the pharmacy.

Walking to the pharmacy put us in the shoes of potential clients who we were trying to help: it shined the spotlight on the terrible process we were trying to fix, especially when we had to purchase large quantities of "climax control" condoms for premature ejaculation and XXL condoms at the counter in front of massive lines of people who can hear and see what you're buying. In Chile, condoms are high up, behind the counter. You must order in front of a long line of people to get the condom you want.

Next, we had to validate that people would buy from a stand-alone website outside of the friendly confines of Mercado Libre, so we setup a landing page using Jumpseller with a 99designs logo and send some Facebook traffic to the site. We saw that people were adding products to their cart, trying to buy. We quickly added DineroMail, a Latin America payment processor that charges 7% fees and holds your money for 1-2 months and started to sell online, still filling orders at the pharmacy.

By this point, we'd spent a total of $300 on 99designs, Facebook ads, and postage filling orders. We'd validated that people wanted to buy condoms online, that they'd buy from a site they didn't know, off Mercado Libre and that we were ready to try to scale the business.

5. Building the Foundation

We decided to spend another $500 for a custom Jumpseller design, purchased $400 of stock of Chile's three best selling condoms (Lifestyles in case you were wondering), wrote 20 educational articles to get organic traffic and officially launched La Condoneria. We launched with the three most popular brands (Lifestyles, Trojan and Durex) and all 24 popular styles you could find at pharmacies even though we only purchased stock of three styles. We priced the other 21 styles we didn't have in stock 50% higher than in the pharmacy so that we could see if people were price sensitive, and also because I was sick of walking to the pharmacy to buy condoms each day.

We saw that we had four distinct niche clients and created content and packs for each one:

1. Young adults between 15-21 who didn't know the first thing about sex and were scared to go to the pharmacy – "First time pack" that included a sex-ed pamphlet that helped people decide if they were ready for their first time and if they were, how to be safe their first time.
2. Women who didn't want to go to the pharmacy because of social stigma – Women's pack, plus dozens of articles about female sex-ed.
3. 24-25 year old men who bought 2-3 months worth of condoms at a time to stock up – Pack "heavy user", a popular 30 pack.
4. "Professionals" who were looking for a good price – "Bulk Pack", a 90 pack, that offered big discounts.

After four months, we'd now purchased all 24 styles and were growing quickly. Our content was incredibly popular, leading to 100k monthly organic traffic, a loyal following and lots of newspaper articles and radio appearances. Our clients loved us because we were really helping people. In a country where most people have incredible misconceptions about sex, abortion in any situation is illegal, getting the morning after pill is very difficult and young people don't really have anyone to talk to about making this important life decision, we were clearly doing good.

Our live chat was incredibly important for two reasons:

1. It became the place for people to go when they had questions about sex and many times we had to refer people to their local clinician or to a specialist to help them solve their problems.
2. We could guide people to purchase our highest margin, best products. If we talked to someone on our chat, they converted at around 33%, whereas we had 1% conversion rates on the site.

By the sixth month in operation, we were selling about $5000 per month, but just breaking even. We were convinced that we had found a good niche, learned how to logistics well and know how to acquire clients cheaply, but we needed to explore other ways to up our margin. We knew that if we continued to sell imported commodity condoms, we'd never do better than a 10% final margin, even at scale.

6. New Opportunities for Scaling Revenue

After a few weeks of brainstorming we came up with this list and worked to validate each one:

1. Take the exclusive representation of a well know, foreign condom brand and get 65% net margins, up from 10%.
2. Create our own white label condom brand and get up to 95% net margins.
3. Add high margin sex toys
4. Convince local condom brands to advertise on the site

We first looked at taking the exclusive representation of a well know, high quality brand. We had multiple meetings in Santiago with an executive from one of the best condom companies in the world, but in the end, he decided to award representation to another, only offline, Chilean business. We talked to a fast growing, well known, US brand that had already launched in Latin America, but it quickly became clear that they didn't understand the Chilean market.

They wanted us to purchase a half container's worth in our first order, and 2 containers worth by year two. Unfortunately, Chile's entire market only uses about 8 containers per year, so we were being asked to purchase 5% of the condoms sold per year in our initial order and then close to 20% by year three. It just didn't make sense. As an aside, Chile's condom consumption isn't low because Chileans are much less sexually active than their neighbors, they just use fewer condoms (under 1 per capita per year, compared to 5 in Uruguay, 4 in Peru and Argentina.)

Next, we looked at manufacturing our own brand and importing. This opportunity was extremely attractive because the unit cost delivered in Chile was about 2 cents, and the final sale price was about $1.20. Massive margins. But the minimums were high and Chile's regulatory barriers were almost impossible to comply with without massive investment. For example, we needed to give the government 10,000 units for testing before we could get the brand registered and we were told off the record that Chile wouldn't approve a new brand that wasn't approved in another developed country in the world.

We looked at adding high margin sex toys, but we didn't think it would work for multiple reasons.

1. Japi Jane, a highly successful online sex toy store, controlled the market.
2. We weren't sure that our clients would purchase many toys.

We did some tests using products we'd purchased on Amazon (I brought them to Chile in my luggage and got a letter saying TSA had opened my baggage for extra security checks), but we couldn't make the numbers work.

We tried to convince local condom brands to pay us, but they all had traditional, conservative views and weren't interested. The best we could do was to negotiate free samples that we could later sell, but it quickly became clear that this method wouldn't work in the long run.

After a year in the business, we were selling $8000 per month with 100% free organic and social traffic, making about 10% net margins and it clearly wasn't worthwhile to keep trying to expand. La Condoneria had turned into a nice small business that will continue to grow, but will never be a massive business.

But it served it's purpose. We learned everything there is to know about Chilean ecommerce and the massive opportunities that entrepreneurs can attack. We decided to spin off La Condoneria to one of my partners who wanted to operate the business to continue to help Chileans buy condoms online, who ran it for another year before shutting it down.

I'm ready to launch my next ecommerce business taking everything we learned from our first La Condoneria to create a highly profitable business.

6. *What we learned*

If you're not going to be Amazon or have millions of dollars of VC to attack payments or drop shipping we believe the opportunities are:

1. Focus on creating your own product, a la Warby Parker
2. Get exclusive representation of a product, like our friend Stephen Stynes did with Pouchee.

Delivery, in Chile, for everything except large items is pretty much solved. On demand delivery will be solved by the extremely well funded UberRush or its competitors. Payments pretty much work. Infrastructure is well executed with Jumpseller and other competitors, plus Shopify will be moving into the rest of Latam eventually.

From our original list in 2012, many of the ideas have been launched:

*   Baby Tuto – $1m+ annual sales of baby products in chile. Have their own branded delivery for large items.
*   Obzes – makeup marketplace, closed in 2014, low margins and shut down.
*   Briu – Coffee subscription club
*   Mangacorta – Custom tshirts, just raised $120k on Broota, a Chilean equity crowdfunding platform, and continues to grow.
*   Pouchee – Purse organizers
*   Linio – Amazon clone from Rocket Internet
*   Dafiti – Zappos clone from Rocket Internet
*   Bike stores – Many
*   Dperfumes – Perfume
*   Adorate – Women's underwear, closed in 2014, low margins, hard to sell online.
*   Depto 51 – Design marketplace

Chapter 10

Visa and Entry Requirements

There are multiple ways you can come to Chile, the most popular being tourist visas, student visas and work visas. This chapter describes the different types of visas and the best way to get them.

Chilean Entrance Visas

It's fairly easy for people from most countries in the world to come to Chile, whether it's as a tourist, a student or a worker. If you plan to come as a tourist and are coming from Europe, North America, Australia, New Zealand, South Africa or most South American countries, you don't need a tourist visa ahead of time. Just show up at the border and you can stay for 90 days. If you are from the US, Mexico, Canada or UK you have to pay a reciprocity fee to enter the country.

If you already have a job or university class lined up, the university or company will likely help you get your one year temporary visa in one of the many Chilean consulates around the world. Start getting your visa two to three months before you're scheduled to come to Chile. If you have an invitation letter, an employment contract or information from your university, it should be fairly straightforward. Chile doesn't have much official corruption, so you don't have to worry about that.

Be prepared to wait 3-8 weeks for your visa to come through. You'll need to collect a few forms to prove you're healthy, not a criminal or a financial risk to Chile, but the process is easy. You'll need to get a letter from your healthcare professional from within the last 30 days saying that you don't have any diseases. You'll also need to document your financial security, university enrollment or a work contract, plus get a certificate from your national police proving you don't have a criminal record. I was told I needed a certificate from the FBI, but they later accepted one from the local police department where I'd lived for the past seven years. They may make you take an AIDS test and have the right to deny you admission if you test positive. The US has a similar outdated law that is enforced unevenly from back when AIDS was an unknown epidemic.

Working Legally and Staying Longer Term

If you came to Chile on a tourist visa, you can renew it by leaving for as little as a few hours and coming back. I know people who have lived in Chile for 5+ years as tourists, taking a trip over the mountains to Argentina or Peru every 90 days. A vacation every three months isn't such a bad idea, is it? If you're from the US, Europe or other first world countries, you can probably enter and leave on a tourist visa pretty much indefinitely if you behave yourself in Chile. I've heard stories of people from Peru, Kazakhstan and others who are able to do this only a few times before they're denied reentry.

If you came to Chile on a tourist visa and want to stay work, the easiest way is to find someone who can extend you a job offer, pending your work visa. This offer can be real, or you can find one of the companies that offer this service for foreigners. Take this contract to the Extranjeria, the Chilean immigration ministry, along with your passport, some photos and a bit more information and you'll have a temporary visa fairly quickly.

After one year, a temporary resident can apply for a permanent resident visa as a worker, business owner, retiree or many more. If don't meet the requirements or prefer to remain a temporary resident, you can apply for a visa extension instead of permanent residence. I had two temporary visas, then applied for my permanent residence as an Investor, because I have a business in Chile.

Chile's immigration policy is one of the most open to foreigners in the world. Chile wants people with talent who won't be a burden on society. If you can prove it, you'll likely be able to stay. Check out how to renew a temporary visa and apply for permanent residence with step-by-step guides in the appendix of this book.

As I mentioned above, many people live nearly full time in Chile on a tourist visa, either leaving the country every 90 days, or paying ~$100 to extend their visa at the department de la Extranjeria. It's a good option if you don't want to go through Chilean bureaucracy, or if you don't know if it's worth your time and effort to get a temporary visa. But there are downsides. Each person should evaluate their circumstances and decide whether they want to get a temporary visa if they plan to stay more than 90 days or if they'd like to take the tourist visa route.

The best options if you choose the tourist renewal route are to take the bus to Mendoza or find cheap flights via Sky or LATAM to Montevideo, Buenos Aires or Lima. If you don't want to travel, you can pay to extend your visa. But you'll likely have to wait in line ~2 hours to do it.

Your second biggest challenge if you stay on a tourist visa is not having a RUT, the Chilean national identity number. It's just like a Social Security Number in the United States except its completely public. You'll need it to do just about anything in Chile. You won't be able to open a bank account, sign up for TV or internet in your apartment, rent most apartments, get discounts at the grocery store, get a credit card, sign up for a phone plan and many other things. You're basically unable to do anything legally with any of the major companies in Chile.

It's very possible to live in Chile without a RUT, I know people who have done it for multiple years.

Here are a few tips and tricks if you're going to go this route:

- Phone – Use Virgin Mobile's Antiplan or Wom's plans. It's the same service as a plan from one of the other companies, but you pay at the beginning of the month instead of at the end. They're the only plan you can get without a RUT.
- TV/Internet – Ask a friend to sign up with their RUT and pay them monthly. Your landlord might be willing to do this.

- Utilities – Make sure your landlord is willing to pay or explains to you how to pay. You won't be able to pay online because you need Chilean credit or debit cards to do it and you can't get those without a RUT.
- Apartments – Rent from someone with experience renting to foreigners or directly from the apartment owner. Avoid real estate agents without foreigner experience if you can. If you need help with your apartment, contact me via www.andesproperty.com, we've helped hundreds of foreigners find the perfect apartment for them in Chile.
- Paying for Things – If you have a US credit card that doesn't have foreign transaction fees, use it to pay for any shared meal and take the cash. That's the cheapest way to bring money to Chile. Also take a look at finding a Chilean or foreigner in Chile who needs dollars in the US or Euros in the EU. They can take pesos out of their Chilean account and give it to you in exchange for a bank transfer to their foreign account or directly to their Paypal. Make sure you know the other person well, as once you transfer them money, you have little to no recourse. Otherwise you'll get charged between $7-$10 every time you take money out of your bank account using an ATM.

Chapter 11

Working in Chile

It's fairly easy to get a work visa in Chile, especially if you find a company that wants to hire you. If you don't have a work visa or don't want to apply for one, you'll likely only be able to work low wage, off the books jobs. If you get a work visa, you either need to work as an independent contractor and send "boletas" or get a contract and be paid a monthly salary, "liquidaciones."

Boletas are the equivalent to working as an independent contractor in the US, where you pay your own taxes. If you work with boletas, you'll get 10% taken out of your pay. You'll likely get some of it back at the end of the year during tax refund season. Contracted workers get liquidaciones. You have to pay taxes into the national health and national retirement system, generally around 15% in total. These are automatically taken out of your liquidaciones, but if you are an independent contractor and getting paid via boletas, you have to send them into Servicio Impuesto Interno (SII), the Chilean Internal Revenue Service.

It seems to be fairly easy to get a decent job in Chile as a foreigner with some skills. If you have a US or European university degree and speak a decent amount of Spanish, there are many opportunities. Pay is much less than in the US or Europe. Between $500.000 (US$900) and $1.500.000 (US$3000) is considered a decent salary for someone without much experience working in a big company. Higher paying specialties like software developers and engineers can make up to $3.000.000 or more if they find a great job.

But as a single person you can get by on $10,000 a year in Chile, live well for US$20,000, very well for US$40,000 and like a king for US$75,000. There are also a multitude of opportunities to work teaching English in Chile. You can either work for a Chilean company or simply post flyers. Teaching English is a great option if you don't speak much Spanish and want to get a job.

The interview process for almost any job generally starts with sending in your resume. A Chilean resume, called a curriculum, has all of your history: where you went to grade school, high school, university, your address, your comuna, phone number, language skills, personal ID numbers, and previous experience. Many times Chileans have 2-3 page resumes. I recommend nothing over 2. As a foreigner I omitted education before university. Chileans use it to weed out people who "don't fit the profile," i.e. come from lower social classes.

If they like you, they'll likely invite you to a group interview with multiple candidates where they'll run you through situations to gauge your logic and people skills. If they still like you, they'll ask you back for a one on one interview where they'll ask more probing personal questions. In the group interview they'll likely give you multiple psychological tests, which I'm fairly sure are illegal in the US and Europe. They give these tests a great deal of weight it seems, which I think is really strange. Some of my best employees would never have passed Chilean psychology tests. Just be ready for it if they ask you to draw a person out in the rain.

Unemployment is generally low in Chile, but the big industries need talented people. Mining, consumer products, fruit/farming, shipping, tourism and wine are big industries. Although there's recently been an uptick in entrepreneurship and small company creation, most people aspire to work in a big company with job security. When you leave a company, you get paid a "finiquito" or severance pay, which is generally calculated by adding up your unused vacation days and a bonus for how long you worked at the company.

Chileans generally work more hours than we do in the US, but get less done. It seems that people like to spend tons of time in the office, take long lunches and put in face time with their bosses. They could get everything done in 6/7 hours, but stay 8/9. There's a massive amount of public holidays (16 in 2013) and Chileans get 3 weeks of vacation each year, but you only get it after you've worked for 1 year, generally.

Coworkers are generally very friendly at work. Many go out to lunch together and most offices celebrate everyone's birthdays. Bosses can be very sexist and gender roles are very much still very traditional. Many times women who clearly were more experienced than I was and knew how to solve a problem better than I did deferred to me to make a decision in the workplace. Chilean women generally take sexual harassment such as worse job assignments, sexual comments etc, in stride or complain to their friends, but hardly anyone really takes further action. Women generally make less than men for the same job, but people rarely talk about it.

Employers ask really personal questions in your interview that would be illegal in the US. Although age/sex/race discrimination is nominally illegal, it doesn't seem to be widely reported or enforced. For example, one of the most popular restaurants in Chile employs only males. That just wouldn't happen in the US. It's common to see help wanted ads that say "se busca señorita" or "looking for young woman" with age and sex in the job description.

Be ready for questions like: marital status, if you're living with a significant other, your religion, where you used to work, what your parents do, where you live, where you went to high school (less likely if you're foreign), if you're divorced, whether you plan to have kids and many more. Many jobs, it won't matter much. But for some conservative places, it does.

If you don't speak much Spanish, you'll likely have two options: working as an english teacher, which can be low paying or a thankless job, or with a startup company that has offices in Santiago. If you're looking for an expat job in Chile, go to **www.MagmaPartners.com/jobs** and you can see a list of some of the best job opportunities for non native Spanish speakers to work with innovative companies.

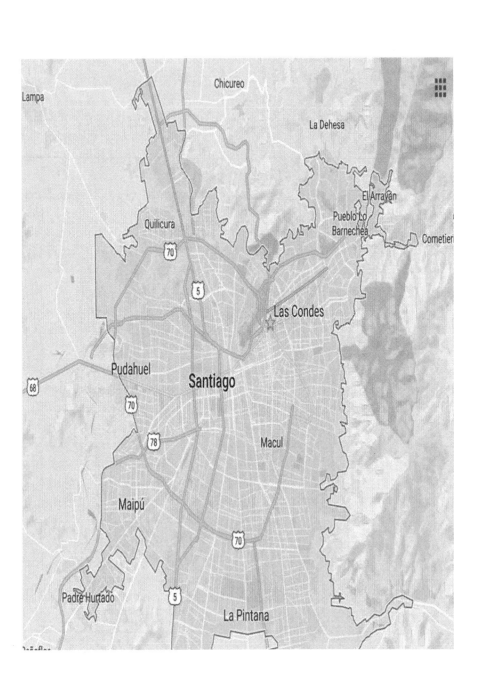

Chapter 12

Apartment Hunting

Ok, so you're coming to Chile. The biggest decision you have to make is where you're going to live. You'll likely be spending the vast majority of your time in the following areas: Santiago Centro, Providencia, Las Condes, Bellavista and Bellas Artes. You may also spend time in Vitacura, Ñuñoa, Recoleta and maybe La Reina. Or you might choose to live outside of Santiago. In many neighborhoods rents have gone up 25-100% from 2010 to 2017 and it's getting harder and harder to find an apartment in the best areas. It's especially difficult to find an apartment that will take a foreigner, much less an apartment that's a good deal.

With the current vacancy rate at around 1%, it's very difficult. Check out Chapter XXX for my Renter's Guide to Chile for the tips and tricks I've used to find my apartments while I've lived in Chile. If you're interested in buying real estate, check out Chapter XXX or www.andesproperty.com my real estate company, for more information.

PROVIDENCIA

The main streets in Providencia are busy, full of people and businesses. It's completely safe during the day and very safe at night. There are restaurants, shopping centers, cafes, all the corporate fast food restaurants, businesses, offices and many high-rise apartments. Once you got off the main streets, Providencia is a leafy, quiet residential neighborhood. I lived at Pedro de Valdivia con Nueva Providencia for 6 months while in Start-Up Chile and, besides for being really close to the main street and a bit noisy, it was perfect.

You're in the middle of everything in Providencia, centrally located and right on the main metro and bus lines. You don't need a car and you can live very well on foot. I never owned a car in six years in Chile, taking the metro, Uber and the occasional rental car to get around. I spend less than owning a car and live hassle free. A furnished one bedroom apartment will run $400,000-$500,000 (US$700-$1000) per month. A two bedroom will cost $475,000-$800,000 (US$900-$1600). Unfurnished tend to be 20-30% less expensive. Apartments are really hot in Providencia right now, so it can be hard to find a place unless you move fast.

If you live in and around Baquedano, you can find cheaper, older apartments that are nice, but not new construction. The area around Baquedano is a little bit more run down, but still fairly safe at night. It has fewer cafés and places to hang out, but is also a good option. The general rule in Providencia is that prices get cheaper the farther you get from a metro stop and the farther south and farther west you go. Prices near Metros Tobalaba and Colon have gone up because Costanera Center, a new mall and movie theater, opened in 2012, making the area more desirable for young upper class professionals.

Another great area close to the office is Barrio Italia. In 2010, it was just starting to redevelop, but by 2017, it's completely changed. Some of the best bars, restaurants and shops are in Barrio Italia. There is a zoning law that restricts building height to 4 stories in Barrio Italia, so finding an apartment can be hard. If you like the area, look just "down" near Metro Santa Isabel and Metro Parque Bustamante. There are more newly built high rise apartments within a short walk to both the office and Barrio Italia.

BELLAS ARTES/LASTARRIA

Near Santiago Centro, these are the artsy, hip areas of Santiago. You'll find some trendy shops, little cafes and none of the corporate chain restaurants you'll find in Las Condes or Providencia. You'll see more adventurous fashion, art house theaters and interesting places to eat. A few years ago Lastarria and Bellas Artes were the up and coming areas, but now they have gone mainstream.

Lastarria is full of apart-hotels, restaurants, bars and tourists. It attracts a different crowd than most of Providencia and can be pricey, but has the most European feel of anywhere in Santiago, with café culture and restaurants spilling out onto the sidewalk.

Bellas Artes is just down from Lastarria and is faster moving, hip and still growing. It's a bit noisier and rougher than Lastarria and a bit cheaper and was one of my favorite places to live in Santiago. The Universidad Católica and Bellas Artes metro stops are right there, making it easy to get around. You're walking distance to cafes, bars, discos, museums, interesting restaurants, Cerro Santa Lucia, downtown, government buildings and Bellavista.

A furnished apartment in Lastarria will cost around the same as one in Providencia, but is harder to find, while one in Bellas Artes will be around the same price as Providencia, but easier to find. If you want to live close by, but want to pay a bit less, you can look down toward Plaza de Armas, where it can be a bit sketchier at night, but still more or less safe. Read more about the Centro in the next section.

Price get a bit lower as you "go down" toward Plaza de Armas , where it can be a bit more dangerous at night, but still relatively safe. Currently, Calle San Antonio and "up" is a fair bit nicer than the area "down" from San Antonio, but the area is getting better fairly quickly.

SANTIAGO CENTRO

Santiago Centro has mostly older buildings, with a few newer ones. It's busy during the day, but clears out rapidly after the workday. Most of the center is safe during the day, but it can get more dangerous at night, mostly because there aren't many people. In 2012, I wrote that I wouldn't live live south of Alameda "down" from Universidad Católica, but as Santiago has improved, these areas have gotten much better too. From 2012-2017 there was a construction boom in Santiago Centro and there are a multitude of brand new highrise apartments with all of the amenities. Prices are lower than Bellas Artes and you're right next to the metro.

If you continue westward toward Barrio Brasil and Barrio Yungay, you'll find cheaper apartments and a nascent foreigner community. I wouldn't live here unless you speak Spanish, but if you do, it's a fun area that's safe during the day, but a bit more dangerous at night.

BELLAVISTA

Bellavista, the area north of Costanera Norte in the shadow of Cerro San Cristobal, is a place where people to go party. It's still very close to multiple metro stops and everything you'd need in the city. In the summer, you'll find people drinking beer at tables lining the main streets and hanging out outside, watching soccer games and chatting. It can be very loud at nights, especially Thursday-Saturday. It's safe during the day, but at night can be a bit dangerous with sketchy people and alcohol from Pio Nono on "downward". Calle Constitución, one block "up" is upscale and much nicer. There are countless bars, places to eat and it's close to Cerro San Cristobal. In 2010, many Chileans poo-pooed Bellavista as a sketchy area, but now it's turned into a go to area of town. There are new high rise apartments and older buildings that have been remodeled and turned into apartments or hostels. Go farther "down" toward Patronato to go even cheaper, edgier, but more dangerous at night ($250,000-$400,000 (US$400-$775) furnished).

LAS CONDES

Las Condes is very safe by day and night. There are three areas in Las Condes where you might choose to live. First, El Golf or "Sanhattan." It's Chile's financial center, hence the nickname, and very upscale. It's the most expensive place in the city to find an apartment and many trendy, expensive restaurants are there. It feels just like parts of LA. The Sanhattan traffic is horrible during rush hour, but if you don't have a car, don't worry. A furnished one to two bedroom apartment will run between $400,000-$800,000

(US$800-$1400), a 3 bedroom apartment $900.000-$1.500.000. and most buildings are very new.

Moving "up", you'll find a bit more reasonably priced apartments near Metro Alcantara. Apartments in these brand new buildings will run $450,000-$650,000 (US$900-$1300). It's quiet, leafy and a close walk to El Golf and great restaurants. It's also right on the metro and will take you 7 minutes to get to the office.

Going farther "up" in Las Condes, you'll find Metro Escuela Militar and then Metro Manquehue. These two areas are filled with heavy traffic and office buildings. There are plenty of chain restaurants, Starbucks and shops. The brand new buildings are very nice and are in the same price range as Alcantara, maybe a bit cheaper. It's a bit farther to the office, but you might find a bit nicer apartment for your money, especially if you look just off the main streets.

Continuing "up" along the metro line, you may find better deals on unfurnished apartments in more residential areas. There are fewer furnished apartments after Metro Manquehue up to Los Dominicos, as they are farther from areas where foreigners generally want to rent.

VITACURA

Vitacura is an upscale, leafy suburb to the northwest of the city. It's quieter, very safe and mostly filled with families. There aren't many individual furnished apartments to rent that aren't incredibly expensive ($600,000-$750,000 (US$1200-$1500), but you can find people renting out spare bedrooms if you really look. Most won't be furnished. You can rent a house cheaper for $600,000-$800,000 ($1200-$1600), but it's very hard for foreigners, as most Chileans want longer term contracts for houses.

You'll find upscale restaurants of varying quality, high-end shops and a completely different environment than the rest of Chile, even Providencia or Las Condes. Vitacura is off the metro line, so you'll need to take colectivos, the bus or get a car. With traffic, it can be as much as an hour to get to Providencia and as little as 15 minutes during off peak hours. If you go another 10 minutes by car north and east, you'll find Lo Barnachea and La Dehesa, the most expensive and upscale suburbs in the city. If you're here with a family, this might be the place for you. Farther out you'll find

Chicureo, a new development about 30 minutes from Santiago (without traffic) with big houses, lots of land and cleaner air. It can be really expensive, as land prices have shot up recently, as much as US$5000 per month for a family house.

OTHER AREAS

Ñuñoa – You can find good deals in Ñuñoa, but most won't be furnished and not many Start-Up Chile participants ventured here. One of my best friends lives here and it's a leafy, safe area of the city, a little bit down the scale from Providencia in terms of construction, price and safety. You won't find many foreigners living here, but it's a nice place to check out, especially if you want to save money. If you're interested in Ñuñoa, check out the areas around Plaza Ñuñoa, Plaza Egaña and just south of Barrio Italia. Many areas are away from the metro, but that will change in 2018, as a new metro line connects Ñuñoa with the rest of Santiago's metro line.

La Reina – A little cheaper and off the beaten path than Vitacura, but more residential than Las Condes or Providencia. It's fairly far from the office, but if you're looking for a quiet place at a lower price it can be an option.

Barrio Brasil and Barrio Yungay – These are two up and coming neighborhoods in central Santiago that are filled with old buildings that are being rehabbed and new buildings that are springing up all over the place. It's cheaper and there's some interesting culture sprouting up, but can be dangerous and a bit drab at night. Check out Concha y Toro, a micro barrio near metro República for interesting up and coming old buildings.

OUTSIDE SANTIAGO

Viña del Mar/Valparaiso – Get out of Santiago, but still close enough that if you need to go for a meeting, you can take a day trip. You can live on the ocean in a slower, cleaner environment with access to good food, beaches and fun parties. Prices are cheaper than in Santiago. Most Start-Up Chile people who lived outside Santiago chose Viña del Mar, or it's smaller neighbor Reñaca.

The South – Pucon, Puerto Varas, Chiloé: Small towns ~10–14 hours south of Santiago by car. Serviced by with frequent flights. Quiet, lakes, nature.

Puerto Varas has grown quickly in the past 4-6 years, as many Santiaguinos have left the city for a slower lifestyle along its beautiful lakeshore.

Antofagasta – If you're working in mining, think about living in Antofagasta

Other cities – I don't really know enough about living in the other cities to make a comment, but if you have questions and are interested in learning more, send me an email and I can connect you with someone who's lived there to give you more information.

TIPS AND TRICKS FOR RENTING

There are many options for both long and short term stays in Chile. For short-term stays, there are always the traditional hotels, but they are generally overpriced compared to the rest of the world. There are many hostels of varying quality for a decent price and the best place to find them is on HostelWorld.com. Airbnb is just starting to get popular in Chile and there are many apartments and houses on the site, but most of them are targeted at foreigners and are expensive. Apart-Hotels are plentiful and range in quality and amenities. Some are similarly priced to a hotel, while others are more reasonable.

Couchsurfing.com is an option and there seems to be an active scene in Santiago. Also check out compartodepto.cl, a resource to facilitate apartment sharing. Another good resource is Facebook. There are a variety of groups where foreigners can look for apartments. You have to wade through the posts to find good deals, but they are there.

It is really difficult to find a place to live in Santiago and it's especially difficult if you are a foreigner. Foreigners don't have all of the paperwork that most Chilean landlords require and Chileans generally prefer to deal directly with other Chilean tenants. Vacancy rates are around 1% and many apartments rent within hours, not days. Homeowners can be very choosy about who they rent to because there are so many people looking for apartments and houses. It's so tight because incomes have risen and more young people are leaving their parents' houses to go and live on their own. Additionally, there are many more foreigners in Chile now than ever before.

If you're staying for a longer period of time, you can rent a furnished apartment/house, an unfurnished apartment/house or share with roommates.

Finding your own apartment is difficult, especially if you don't speak Spanish.

Expect to find "gringo prices" if you call a real estate agent and speak poor Spanish. When I first moved to Chile I called an apartment owner using my at the time broken Spanish. He quoted me $400,000 (US$800) for an unfurnished one bedroom apartment. It was way too expensive. I had a Chilean friend call later that afternoon and he quoted $250,000 (US$500). My example is drastic, but expect people to try to charge you an extra 10-25%.

It's customary that the individual renter, rather than the landlord, pays all bills while he's living there. Normally apartments are priced as the rent, plus gastos comunas, or building fees. These can be anywhere from $35,000 (US$70) to $100,000 (US$200) per month, depending on apartment size, amenities and whether the building has any major issues. Be sure to ask about gastos comunas up front. You'll likely be expected to pay cable, Internet, hot and cold water, electricity and gas, but some apartments have their utilities paid out of gastos comunas. This is both good and bad. If you use lots of resources, the rest of the tenants will subsidize you, but if you use few, you'll end up paying more than you otherwise would.

Most landlords will force you to sign at least a one-year contract, but some of the furnished apartments can be had for 3-6 month commitments at higher rates. You're expected to pay a half a month's rent to the property manager for helping you find your apartment when you sign your contract, even if they did nothing more than show you the place. You'll also be expected to pay at least one month's deposit, sometimes two, so be prepared to have 3-4 months rent available when you're signing a lease.

A typical monthly apartment will have the following costs:

Rent
Gastos Comunas (building fees)
Water
Electricity
Gas
Parking (if not included)
Cleaning (if you hire a maid)
Internet/TV

Rent plus gastos comunas are very important to know ahead of time, as sometimes landlords will try to hide high gastos comunas to get you to pay higher rent. Try to see bills from previous months for the other services so you can calculate the true monthly cost of an apartment. Be sure to visit your apartment during a busy time in the neighborhood.

I visited my first apartment in Santiago on a Sunday and the apartment was perfect: quiet, on a plaza, close to the metro, close to a bus stop, grocery store, good views. But after I moved in I realized local musicians asking for money played in the plaza every day from 4-11pm and that the small bus stop in front of my house was in fact a major stop on weekdays, complete with incredibly loud city busses. Another friend of mine rented an apartment on a Sunday and didn't notice the construction site right next door. Welcome to early morning pile driving! Another visited his apartment during the day and didn't notice that the strip club across the street had a massive neon red sign that gave his apartment a nice shade of red at night.

It's really hard to find an apartment that's a good value, in a decent location that will rent to foreigners. It took me two months to find my apartment and I had the flexibility to go to see apartments during the day. Other friends have taken longer or ended up settling for an apartment that was just ok, or was overpriced. During my search, I found multiple apartments that I wanted, talked to the landlord or property management company and thought I had it in the bag. Chilean landlords will ask for lots of paperwork. It's not as easy as just giving them a check for a few months' rent and they give you the keys. Since the vacancy rate is under 1% and all apartments get tons of prospective tenants, the owners can be choosy. They'll likely ask you for the following paperwork:

- Copy of Chilean ID or Passport
- Contract to work in Chile. If you've just been hired at a known company, this may be all you need.
- Copies of previous work/salary history. They'll only recognize Chilean payments validated by the government.
- A Chilean credit report. Copy of your bank accounts, both in Chile and abroad Anything else a landlord might be able to think of

When I my rent, but didn't have many payments in Chile because I was going back and forth to the US. I sent a copy of my bank account in Chile that showed assets and an impeccable credit report, but after the property management company "checked my paperwork" they always told me they'd rented the apartment to someone else. It was so frustrating. They didn't care about assets, only income or a contract.

The only apartments I could find whose owners were interested in renting to foreigners were furnished apartments that rented almost immediately. You can use a service to help you find your apartment, but expect to pay at the top of the market, or more expensive than you could find on your own. Also expect to pay at least 50% of the first month's rent to the agency that helps you. Many of them will make you pay that fee again after 6 or 12 months if you want to renew the lease.

This is the protocol I used to search for my apartment:

- Decide if you want furnished or unfurnished tried to rent, I had assets in Chile and could prove that I could pay
- Walk around the areas you like and look for signs. Stop in to buildings you like and ask the concierges if there are any spaces available.
- Search on Portal Inmobilario and Propiedades Emol. New properties come out each day, so sort by property code to get the newest apartments
- Look for apartments for rent by owner
- Call the number in the ad immediately and try to go see the apartments during lunch or the early afternoon
- If you want an apartment, decide right away. Talk with the owner and sell them that you're a stable potential tenant.
- Have all of your paperwork ready and send it immediately
- Be ready to sign quickly
- If you don't speak Spanish, consider asking a friend or paying one of the services to help you.

ANDES PROPERTY

Note: This is a blatant advertisement/self promotion for my apartment rental business that I started with a Start-Up Chile alumni in 2012. Since then, we've helped hundreds of foreigners find apartments in Chile. If you need help finding an apartment, our team would be happy to help! You can find us at AndesProperty.com or email us directly, contact@andesproperty.com.

When I first got to Chile in 2010 as part of the pilot round of Start-Up Chile, my first task, just like yours will be, was to find an apartment. We reserved a hostel for the first week, and set out to rent an apartment.

It was a daunting task. I spoke a bit of Spanish, but my business partner Jesse didn't really speak much at all. We started looking for shared apartments, furnished apartment rentals and unfurnished units in Providencia, Las Condes and Bellas Artes, but were quickly stymied. We didn't really know where to search, our Spanish wasn't up to snuff and even when we did find a decent property, many landlords either didn't want to rent to foreigners or jacked up the rent 2-3x when they heard my broken Spanish. They also asked us for paperwork that we didn't have and we quickly realized that unless we were planning on staying for more than a year, buying furniture, which isn't deductible from your Start-Up Chile grant, didn't make sense.

After looking for a few days, we thought we'd found the apartment we wanted right near Metro Pedro de Valdivia. The photos were amazing. It had a pool. Two bedrooms. A balcony facing the Andes. I called and asked for the price and a time to go see it. When we got there and walked in, I knew we'd been taken for a ride. It was a one bedroom studio that was in no way close to what we'd seen online.

When another apartment quoted me $1500/month, I asked my Chilean friend Cristóbal to call and try to rent it. His quote? $700. They'd tried to gringo tax us! Other apartments just flat out told us they wouldn't rent to us unless we could show a year of income in Chile, have permanent residency, and have a Chilean cosigner.

We ended up using an agency that worked out ok, but we ended up paying extra rent and having to put four months as a down payment. Other friends weren't so lucky and ended up getting taken advantage of by unscrupulous brokers.

Many of our friends ended up paying way over market value or having to pay their entire lease up front. And forget about getting your security deposit back at the end of your lease! Most of our friends ended up losing nearly all of their deposit and had no recourse. It turns out that for most Chileans the idea of a security deposit is really a "I use your money as an extra month's rent" deposit!

In 2012 when I first moved back to Chile, I decided to start to solve the problem. One of my fellow Pilot round Alumni and I decided to create

Andes Property, a company dedicated to helping foreigners find apartments to rent with a US level of customer service, fully bilingual service and without the typical Chilean paperwork and demands.

We started by buying our own apartments in Bellas Artes and then have taken over management of Chilean owned apartments that allow us to rent to foreigners using our standards. If you're looking for an apartment, shoot us a message. We'd be happy to help you out.

You can find us at AndesProperty.com or email us directly, contact@ andesproperty.com. End of Blatant Self Promotion.

Real Estate Investing

Chile is an attractive place for investing in real estate. Property rights are strong, property taxes are low and you can find properties that generate significant returns, or make sense to buy for your primary residence. Rents have risen significantly all over Chile since 2009 and so have the real estate prices. In many areas of the city, your monthly mortgage payment on an apartment or house is less than you would pay in rent if you were able to get a loan to purchase a property. The biggest jumps in prices have happened in Las Condes, Vitacura, La Dehesa and parts of Providencia. Other areas have seen increases, but not as significant.

Chile's economic growth is building a significant middle class that wants to live in nice, interesting apartments. Additionally, The New York Times named Santiago the best place to travel in 2011 and the Start-Up Chile program has attracted thousands of foreign business people to live in Chile. There's at least a 98% occupancy rate in areas where you'd want to think about living.

Many areas are still underpriced by historical data, while the aforementioned areas are closer to market price and some are even entering into potential bubble territory. It can be attractive for a foreigner to purchase property in Chile, although it can be tricky to bring your money into Chile without paying taxes and to make sure that you're buying a property that's free and clear, and that the seller has the right to actually sell.

Always buy property with the help of an attorney, ideally one with experience helping foreigners purchase properties. Banks will generally ask for between 10-20% down and will require you to show income documents and be a permanent resident in order to get a loan. The banks will want to see that your income is 3-4x higher than the monthly loan payment will be.

Besides for apartments and houses in Santiago, there are many opportunities to purchase a beach house, farmland, a vacation house in the south or a cabin in the mountains. Chile has incredible natural beauty, and purchasing property can be a great way to experience it and own a great investment. Chile has very solid property rights, very low property taxes (as low as ~$150 a year on a $100,000 property), low interest rates and good landlord rights if you intend to rent the property out. I own multiple properties and have helped foreigners avoid the usual pitfalls when purchasing properties on their own.

If you're interested in purchasing property, check out www.andesproperty.com for more information. We've helped foreigners find, evaluate, purchase and rent out properties all over Chile and currently own and manage hundreds of apartments. Our team is happy to help you get your head around the market and see if investing in Chilean real estate makes sense.

Chapter 13

Santiago City Guide

Santiago is an interesting city in that each area is very different; You'll have a markedly different experience depending on where you're going to eat, relax or party. This chapter's subsections contain lists of some of my favorite places in each comuna, along with brief descriptions on what to expect when going out in each one.

SECTION 1

Restaurant Guide

Although the Chilean food scene, especially in Santiago, has improved by leaps and bounds since 2010, you need to diligently search in order to find them. You can't choose a random restaurant and expect it to be good... you should probably expect it to be pretty poor. Google doesn't help much unless you know restaurant names and TripAdvisor has restaurants that are mostly touristy. Your best bet is to find a local with similar taste and get their recommendations. Check <u>http://www.nathanlustig.com/2015/04/26/chile-restaurant-guide-best-restaurants-in-chile/</u> for my most up to date recommendations.

Here's what I've uncovered in my time here:

Brunch

Ensaladeria Holm – Padre Mariano 125. Providencia. Huge Saturday and Sunday brunches. Fresh fruit and vegetable juices and smoothies. Salads and sandwiches during the week. $$$.

Casa Zucca – Presidente Riesco 3006. El Golf. Old house with a beautiful courtyard tucked away from busy El Golf. Small menu, but large portions and high quality food. Great for a relaxing Saturday brunch, closed on Sunday. $$.

Thai

Pad Thai – Manuel Montt 231. Providencia. Solid Thai Restaurant with a cool courtyard. The Pad Thai is great, other main dishes are decent. Appetizers and desserts are a bit lacking, but main dishes are really good. $$$.

Thai House – Manuel Montt 1020. Providencia. Authentic Thai food a bit farther down Manuel Montt than Pad Thai. The décor isn't as cool as Pad Thai. Most dishes are better here except I prefer the Pad Thai and ambiance at Pad Thai. Try the green tea cake with melted white chocolate for dessert. $$$.

Indian

Rishtedar – Holanda 160. Providencia. Real authentic Indian food. Huge menu. Many vegetarian options. One of my favorite restaurants in Santiago. Try the mushroom appetizer, the authentic naan and spicy curry. If you want it spicy like Indian food should be, you have to ask for it, as Chileans don't tolerate spice well. Delivery for $2.000. $$$.

New Horizon – Merced 565. Bellas Artes. Authentic Indian food. Small menu, small restaurant. I love the fish curry. Cheap lunch specials. Great value. $.

Vegetarian

El Naturista – Huerfanos 1046 & Moneda 846. Centro. Rosario Norte 532 Las Condes. Vegetarian restaurant with two locations close to Universidad de Chile metro. Great pebre (tomatoes, cilantro, onions, goes on bread) which goes really well with all of their dishes. My favorite is huevos rancheros with tons of pebre. $$.

El Huerto – Orrego Luco 54. Providencia. My favorite salads in Santiago. Their homemade whole wheat bread and their very vegetabley pebre are great. Meat eaters, try Nuevo Mexico, you'll almost forget you're not eating meat. $$$.

Quinoa – Luis Pasteur 5393. Vitacura. A vegetarian's dream, reasonably priced, especially for the area, top-notch food in a cool location. They also have great brunch. $$$.

Shakti – Av Italia 1568. Barrio Italia. Vegan. Interesting food, even for meat eaters. The interpretation of ceviche but made with mushrooms instead of fish is really good. $$.

Rishtedar. See the Indian food section. Many vegetarian options.

Sandwiches

La Gloria – Huerfanos casi esquina Amunategui, Santiago Centro and Manuel Montt 1315, Providencia. Peruvian sandwich shop. Amazing service, top quality food. Might be my favorite sandwiches in Chile. Love the fish sandwich with the spicy sauce. $.

Fuente Alemana – Pedro de Valdivia 210 and Bernardo O'Higgins 58 (near Plaza Italia). The best lomitos in Santiago. Huge sandwiches. A completo comes with lettuce, tomato, sauerkraut, avocado, mayo. Add spicy mustard for extra kick. Kind of touristy, but worth it every once in awhile. $$.

Dominó – Multiple Locations. Not to be confused with the US pizza chain, Dominó is my go to fast food restaurant. It's how fast food should be. Good ingredients, lots of choices, not expensive. They have surprisingly good salads as well. For a change of pace: get the vegetarian sandwich (avocado, tomato, cheese) with a "paila" of eggs. $.

Donde Guido – Bellas Artes. Peruvian sandwich shop with lots of interesting sauces. Fast, good, filling. Big sandwiches…you won't go away hungry. $.

La Superior – Nueva de Lyon 105. Providencia. Upscale versions of Chilean classic sandwiches. One of the best beer lists in the city with 25+ Chilean brewed beers. Packed for lunch, but easy to get a table for dinner. $$$.

Elkika – Multiple locations in Providencia. Big, tasty sandwiches, cheap beer. Always packed. A local favorite. $$.

Aleman Experto – Two locations in Providencia. Good German sandwiches for a solid price. $$.

Pizza

Tiramisu – Isidora Goyenechea 3141. El Golf. Great thin crust pizza. Reasonably priced for location, cool atmosphere and top-notch food. It's always packed, no matter when you go. Expect to wait if you go during peak hours. Have a pisco sour while you wait at the bar. The ice cream is extremely underrated. $$$.

Fabrica de Pizza – Bellavista. Lower quality, but good thin crust pizzas for US$6-9 and cheap beer. A place to sit outside on a nice sunny day or a warm night with a bunch of guys. Cheap and "interesting" people watching. $.

Caperucita – El Bosque Norte 083. El Golf. Thin crust pizza with interesting combinations. Also has delivery.

Ciudadano. Barrio Italia. Seminario 400. Thin crust pizza, Chilean food and a great atmosphere. Nice place to go out with friends. $$$.

Korean

Sukine – Antonia Lopez de Bello 244. Patronato. One of my favorite restaurants in the city. Authentic Korean food with owners who barely speak Spanish. Really cheap, a great place to go with groups. Best for lunch or early dinner, as neighborhood can be sketchy at night. $$.

Vietnamese

Vietnam Discovery – Loreto 324. Patronato. One of the only Vietnamese restaurants in Santiago. Great food, sophisticated decoration. $$$.

Peruvian

Barandiaran – Manuel Montt 315. Providencia. Patio Bellavista and Nuñoa. Manuel Montt is my favorite location they converted a beautiful old house into the restaurant with a large courtyard. Great food, classic Peruvian. Really strong pisco sours. Great place for a special occasion. I love the corvina with mango sauce and shrimp and the filete a lo macho, along with the ceviche. $$$$.

El Encuentro Peruano – Ismael Valdés de Vergara 790. Santiago Centro. A Peruvian restaurant that caters to Peruvians who are living in Chile.

Affordable, big portions, strong pisco sours, good flavor, cool old building. My favorite affordable Peruvian restaurant. $$.

Astrid y Gastón – Antonio Bellet 201. Providencia. From world renown chef Gaston Acurio. Intricate, flavorful, Peruvian food. One of the most expensive restaurants in the city. Only for special occasions or if your parents are visiting (and paying!). $$$$$.

La Mar – Nueva Costanera 3922. Vitacura. Rivals Astrid y Gastón as the top Peruvian restaurant in the city. Better ambiance and outdoor seating, known for its seafood and ceviches. The only Peruvian with vegetarian menu, but you have to ask for it specially. For special occasions. $$$$$.

Japanese

Shoo-gun – Enrique Foster Norte 172. El Golf. Authentic Japanese restaurant with interesting Japanese dishes, other than sushi. Good sushi, but expensive. I love the katsundun, a rice, pork, egg and onion bowl. Lunch menu is a great value. $$$$.

Sushi

Goeman – Manuel Montt 37. Providencia. The best, most authentic Japanese restaurant in Santiago. If you're used to Chilean style sushi with avocado and cream cheese, you might not like Goeman, but it's incredibly good. Might need reservations, has small capacity. $$$$.

Kintaro – Monjitas 460. Bellas Artes. Fairly priced, great rolls, least use of cream cheese in their sushi in Santiago. Sashimi is good, but not spectacular. Try a sushi boat sample platter if you go with friends. $$$.

Senz – Cerro Plomo 5680 Las Condes and Costanera Center Tobalaba. Peruvian inspired sushi. Large sushi rolls with interesting Peruvian inspired sauces and fillings. I prefer the Las Condes location, as it's quieter. Really busy for lunch. $$$.

Zabo – Dardignac 0191. Bellavista. A bit expensive for what you get, but really good, high quality sushi. Great sashimi. Good drink menu. $$$.

Bushido – Francisco Bilbao 399, Barrio Italia. Las Condes 9377. Las Condes. Great sushi with interesting combinations, but terrible Thai food. The contrast between the quality sushi and the garbage worthy Thai food is incredible. Go for the sushi. Don't be tempted to try the Thai. Good delivery. $$$.

Chilean

Peumayen – Constitución 136. Bellavista. Peumayen's tagline is "ancestral food" and is the first restaurant in Chile that's honoring Chile's rich indigenous food tradition. I foreigners here whenever they come to visit Chile, as it's an experience. Start with a North to South bread sampler, an appetizer platter to share and a unique main dish, all in a beautifully restored Chilean house. Expensive, but worth it for a special occasion. $$$$.

Divertimiento Chileno – Pedro de Valdivia Norte at Cerro San Cristóbal. High quality Chilean food. Expensive, but a great location surrounded by trees in the park at the foot of Cerro San Cristóbal. You may need a reservation at night or during lunch. $$$$.

La Casa de Don Benito – Camino Lonquen Norte Parcela 16. Lonquen. Located about 30 minutes from downtown Santiago, Don Benito serves classic Chilean food and claims to have the best empanadas in all of Chile. The no frills food is excellent and all of his restaurants are packed on weekends. $$.

La Piojera – Aillavilú 1030. Metro Cal y Canto. Santiago Centro. La Piojera is a bit like going back in time, before tv, before radio and electricity. It's what I image our great great grandfathers did in their spare time after a hard day's work. It's a divey traditional place famous for their terremotos, which are drinks made of white wine, pineapple sorbet and some light liquor. The meat on the bone and the hot sauce is great, but the place is dirty and if you think too hard, its gross. A place to go for drinks and brave the food. Although it's getting touristy, it's still worth going at least once for the experience. Really cheap. Half a dollar sign.

Salvador Cocina y Café – Bombero Ossa 1059. Santiago Centro. Hidden just off of Paseo Ahumada, this restaurant is about 3 blocks from the Universidad de Chile metro and has great homemade lunch. Much better quality for a similar price compared to many of the small restaurants in the center. Try the iced tea. $$.

Liguria – Three locations Pedro de Valdiva, Manuel Montt, Tobalaba. Providencia. Bar and sandwich shop that serves good Chilean food, sandwiches and decent drinks. Food is good, specials are great. Drinks can be expensive for what you get, but it's one of the only bars that serves food after about 12am in Providencia. $$$.

Juan y Medio – Barrio Brasil, Rancagua and Vitacura. Originally a truck stop about an hour south of Santiago that served massive portions of hearty, classic Chilean food. Now Juan y Medio has up locations in Santiago. It's hit and miss: sometimes its really tasty, other times not great. $$$.

Galindo – Dardignac 098, Bellavista. Cheap Chilean food. Good place for beers and chorrillana with friends or Sunday lunch with a group or traditional chilean food after work during the week. $$.

J Cruz – Condell 1466. Valpariaso. The original chorrillana: Artery cloggin' french fries, grilled onions and meat. Accompanied by a beer. The location oozes history and is down a dark alley. But it's worth it if you've made the trip to Valparaiso. $.

Las Cabras – Luis Thayer Ojeda 0116, Providencia. High quality Chilean classics at an updated version of a Chilean "fuente de soda" or soda fountain. Smallish portions but very high quality food. $$.

Bar Nacional. Centro, El Golf. Huge menu of Chilean classics. Good value for money. Packed at lunch, good place for after work drinks. $$$.

Tip y Tap. Multiple Locations. German/Chilean food. Good place for a solid business lunch.

Seafood

Portofino – Bellamar 301, Cerro Esperanza, Valparaiso. Top-notch seafood on the coast. The incredible views alone are probably worth the price of the meal. Good wine list, great service. $$$$.

Punta Mai – Avenida del Mar 1366, Maitencillo. Located about two hours north of Santiago, Punta Mai has great seafood in an upscale atmosphere. A bit expensive, but if you're already on the coast, its worth it. $$$$.

Mercado Central – Metro Cal y Canto. Mercado Central is a bit of a tourist trap, but it really does have great seafood. Don't order the crabs, they're insanely expensive. The best tip here might be to purchase fresh seafood and cook it at your house. It's way cheaper and more fun to look at all the interesting fish and shellfish that you probably haven't seen before. $$-$$$$.

See: *Peruvian restaurants* – They usually have great seafood.

Meat

Las Vacas Gordas – Cienfuegos 280. Barrio Brasil. A traditional Chilean parrillada and meat restaurant. Huge, open grill that you can see right as you walk in. Great pisco sours and desserts. A great place for Saturday lunch, but expect to wait a bit. $$.

Ox – Nueva Costanera 3960. Vitacura. Some of the best meat in Santiago. Expensive, good wine list, great appetizers, but worth it for a special occasion. $$$$$.

Happening – Av. Apoquindo 3090. El Golf. Rivals Ox in quality, but a little less expensive. Good value for money on the meat, but sides and wine can be expensive. $$$$.

Eladio. Nueva Providencia 2250, piso 5. Also locations in Bellavista and La Reina. One of the best value for money bets in Santiago. Quality meat dishes, strong, affordable pisco sours, good wine. $$.

Gringo

California Cantina – Las Urbinas 56. Providencia. Gringo bar with burgers, texmex food and moderately priced drinks. Decent, not great, but if you're craving a US atmosphere, go here. Great place to watch US or European sports on TV. $$$.

The White Rabbit. Antonia Lopez de Bello 0118. Bellavista. Small bar/restaurant based on US hipster restaurants. $$$.

Italian

Golfo da Napoli – Dublé Almeyda 2435. Ñuñoa. The best value for money Italian restaurant in Santiago. It's cheap, has huge portions and has the feel as if you've been transported right over to Europe. The gnocchi melts in your mouth. House wine in US$4 for a half liter. There will likely be a wait on weekends. $$.

Da Noi – Av. Italia 1791. Barrio Italia. Reasonably priced Italian food in Barrio Italia. Waiters bring warm bread with meat-sauce when you arrive. Try the lasagna. $$$.

Fusion

Lusitano – Condell 1414. Barrio Italia. Good food, great tiramisu for dessert. One of the best outdoor terraces in Santiago. Great place for a relaxing lunch or a nice night out with friends or a date.

Étnico – Constitución 172, Bellavista. A loungy type bar/restaurant with great seafood and a top wine list. The food is a bit expensive, but the wine and drinks are fairly priced. Great place to relax with some friends or to take a date. $$$.

Ky – Peru 631. Recoleta. One of my favorite places in the city. Located in an old house filled with old furniture, this is another great place to take a date. Interesting Asian/Chilean dishes, great seafood and a drink menu that's 3x longer than the actual menu. A rare place with character in Santiago. Make sure to make a reservation on weekends. $$$.

Casa Luz – Av. Italia 805. Barrio Italia. Beautifully restored old house with one of the best courtyards in Santiago. Great for a weekend lunch. High quality food, but a bit expensive for what you get. $$$$.

Chipe Libre – Lastarria 282. Lastarria. Food is a bit expensive for what you get. Great place for a drink, as they specialize in interesting pisco drinks. Can be a bit touristy. Look for a seat on the back patio.

Burgers

La Burguesía – Santa Magdalena 99. Providencia. Burger restaurant with interesting mixes of meat and non-traditional toppings. Only outdoor seating. $$$.

Uncle Fletch – Dardignac 0192. Bellavista. The best burgers in Santiago. Brioche bun, high quality meat, crispy bacon, top notch beer list. $$$.

Ice Cream & Desserts

Emporio la Rosa – Parque Forestal and various locations. The best ice cream in the city. Thick, creamy, delicious. My favorite flavor is chocolate avellana (hazelnut). They also have cakes and coffee. The Parque Forestal is the classic location. Grab an ice cream and eat in the park. $$.

Freddo – Costanera Center, 5th floor, Providencia. Parque Arauco, Las Condes. Argentina's favorite ice cream chain comes to Chile. A little piece of Argentina in Chile. $$.

Pastelería Laura R – Manuel Montt 747 and other locations, Providencia, Vitacura. Traditional Chilean cakes, cookies and pastries. Incredible cheese-cake. $.

El Bombón Oriental – Merced 353. Bellas Artes. Traditional Chilean cakes, Turkish coffee. Really nice waitstaff. Has a patio where you can sit outside and enjoy your snack. $.

Le Flaubert – Orrego Luco 125 Providencia. They have delicious small sandwiches, interesting cakes and cookies. Great place for tea and a snack. $$.

Dulceria Las Palmas – El Bosque Sur 42 and various locations. Try to the bite sized cake assortment. $$$.

Toldo Azul – Isidora Goyenechea 3200. El Golf. Premium, interesting favored ice cream. $$.

Moritz-Eis. El Golf, Vitacura, Cachagua. Premium ice cream from Austrian ice cream chef. $$$.

Uruguayan

La Parrilla Uruguaya – Condell 566. Providencia. Second location in Ñuñoa. Amazing meat, feels like you're in Montevideo or Buenos Aires. Cheap beer, wine and drinks. Split a parrillada that comes with a chicken breast stuff with sausage and choose, multiple types of sausage and steak. As a bonus, it's a good place to watch a soccer game. $$.

Sandwicheria La Rambla – Tabancura 1344. Vitacura. Uruguyan sandwiches, specializing in chivitos. $$.

Spanish

De la Ostia – Orrego Luco 065. Providencia. Spanish tapas bar. Solid food. Tasty sangria. Always packed, which sometimes leads to slow service. Good place for a drink with friends. $$$.

Ruca Bar. Condell 868. Barrio Italia. Spanish inspired small plates. Great place for a drink and conversation.

French

Le Flaubert – Santa Magdalena 80. Providencia. Traditional French restaurant with French owners and waiters. Love the beef bourguignon. Most of the time you'll need a reservation. $$$.

Normandie – Providencia 1234. Providencia. Tasty, well prepared French food. Good wine list. Serves pâté and butter with warm bread when you arrive. Cool interior that look like a Paris cafe. $$$.

Boulevard Lavaud (Peluquería Francesa) – Compañía de Jesús 2789. Barrio Brasil. Solid french menu in an old house turned into a restaurant. Still has a functioning old style barber shop in the building in the front. Good food, great place for a date. Really cool décor. $$$.

Baco. Nueva de Lyon 113. Providencia. Upscale (for Chile) French food. Never disappoints, but can be easy to run up a bill if drinking and eating. $$$$.

SECTION 2

Drinking and Going Out

Orrego Luco – Providencia. This is a small street just of Av. Providencia near Pedro de Valdivia that has about 8 bars with outdoor tables. It's full every night, except Sundays. Almost every bar has 2×1 drinks until 12am.

Any outdoor bar on Pio Nono – Bellavista. There are tons of bars with plastic red tables and chairs. You can get a litre of beer for US$2-3 and hang out with friends. You'll see all sorts of characters walking by, but be wary of anyone who starts randomly talking to you in English right away. They are likely shady.

Most of the bars on Manuel Montt, just south of Av. Providencia. There are many bars and restaurants on Manuel Montt that compete for your business. The outdoor ones have the best settings, but the smaller ones have the best drink deals.

El Kika – Providencia/Pedro de Valdivia. Ok, so this is less than a 2 minute walk from my apartment, but it's got good beer, cheap food and lots of outdoor seating. One of my friends asked me "how can you possibly live there, I'd be at El Kika everyday!"

California Cantina – Providencia. Gringo bar with Californian owners. They always show all of the US sports on TV and have decent texmex food. They celebrate all the US holidays there too. A bit expensive compared to other places nearby.

Subterraneo – Providencia. Underground disco right in orrego luco. It's great when they have parties there, but the rest of the time it's dead. Always ask to see inside before you enter, as it can be completely empty.

De la Ostia – Providencia. Spanish themed tapas restaurant with good drinks. Sangria is a good deal and tasty.

Amanda – Vitacura. The "best" club in Chile. Expect a great looking, but conservative crowd. They have special shows with international bands 2-3 times per week and you can buy tickets online. Cover is going to run US$6-$14 depending on the night.

Uracas – Vitacura. Another top club. Crowd is a bit less conservative than Amanda, depending on the night can be a bit younger. There's a strip of bars surrounding it, so you have lots of choices of places to pregame.

Eve – Vitacura. On Wed/Thurs when there are parties it can be really fun, other nights it's dead.

Teclados – Vitacura. There are two locations, the "upper" one is for mostly 18-21 year olds and isn't that great, the "lower" one is an awesome bar with a very mixed crowd. Great french fries.

Ruca Bar – Great place for a drink in Barrio Italia.

White Rabbit – US style atmosphere in Bellavista.

Ciudadano – Good place for food and drink in Barrio Italia.

La Fuente – Vitacura. Mixed crowd, decent food, cheaper drinks.

Bar Esquina – Vitacura. Overpriced, food that's just "ok" but a nice terrace in the summer.

Restaurant Metropol – Vitacura. One of the best places to get a beer in Santiago. They have artisanal Belgian beer and great sandwiches named after metro stops.

Onaciu – Bellavista. One of my favorite places to go out. One of the only places in the city with a mixed crowd. It gets upper class people wanting to break their routine, interesting people from Bellas Artes and Lastarria, plus students. There's two dance floors and it usually has live music 3-4 times per week. Great music, no regeton. US$10-$20 cover.

Bar Loreto – Bellavista. Across the street from Onaciu. Fun crowd, small club. The bar is really cool looking, but its underground and after a bit you'll feel a bit trapped.

Clandestino – Bellavista. Smaller club, mixed crowd, cheap, strong drinks. Good place to dance. People are very easy to talk to. US$6-$10 cover.

Bar Constitiucion – Bellavista. Used to be one of the best places in the city, but still very fun. A mix of foreigners and Chileans looking to meet each other. Two rooms of music, plus a place to chill out.

Patio Bellavista – Bellavista. A bit expensive, this place is a tourist trap. A fun place to grab a drink with friends, but its way cheaper to go around the corner and pick a traditional Chilean place.

Santo Remedio – Providencia. Cool bar with a great drink selection and interesting interior design. Great place to start the night.

Maestro Vida – Bellavista. Salsa club. Middle class crowd and everyone is open to dancing with everyone else. Don't know salsa? No problem, someone there will be happy to teach you.

Any bar in Lastarria – Lastarria. Walk along Calle Lastarria and walk into bars that look interesting. They have interesting drinks, a mixed crowd and interesting food.

El Diablito – Lastarria. An old style Chilean bar, cheap drinks, decent food. Cozy atmosphere, good music.

GOING OUT BY COMUNA

Vitacura

Vitacura is the "high class", rich part of Santiago. The "best" clubs are located here and by best I mean "good looking people", expensive covers and drinks. I use " " here because "high class, best and good looking" are all things that Chileans would say, but if you're a foreigner you may not care about or notice. There are certainly money differences, but much of it is classism. If you want to hookup with someone for the night, it's probably not the place to go. People are more conservative, more worried about their reputation. Girls will likely not introduce themselves to you, but it does happen from time to time. If you want to dance with a girl, you must ask "quieres bailar" (want to dance?) or something similar. Don't just start dancing near a girl like in the US or Europe, you'll get a funny look and have no success.

It's rare to see people making out in the club. You can get a phone number or a Facebook to start to WhatsApp or figure out another time to go out, a coffee date or invite them to a bbq later.

Las Condes

Similar to Vitacura, but the most popular places are the high end bars near El Golf/Escuela Militar and Manquehue More foreigners than Vitacura.

Providencia

As you move lower (west), people are more relaxed, a bit more liberal. Prices are cheaper, people are good looking and fun. Girls are more relaxed and are more likely to introduce themselves or start chatting with you. Guys are a bit more aggressive than in Vitacura, but still generally treat women well. If you're looking for a more relaxed night and with a better chance of picking someone up, go out here.

Bellas Artes & Lastarria

Fairly calm, trendy places to go out. There are bars with more adventurous mixed drinks, a bit more expensive than other bars in the center. Many places are much more gay friendly than other areas in Santiago. Walk along Calle Lastarria or de la Barra and pop into different places that look interesting. Lastarria is fairly touristy and more expensive than other places in the centro. There aren't many clubs, but many more bars here. You can have a fun night starting out drinking in bars here and then heading over to clubs in Bellavista.

Bellavista

Bellavista is a really fun place to go out. People are more relaxed, open and happy to strike up a conversation. Some places can be touristy and others can be very Chilean, depending on where you go. It's probably the best place to go if you're looking to pickup someone. Most places are very safe, but if you get really drunk, you could run into a low class Chilean who'd enjoy messing with a foreigner. I've never had any problems, but it can happen. There is a very distinct difference between the bars and restaurants on Calle Constitucion, which are filled with upscale bars and restaurants, and the establishments on Pio Nono, one block "down" which are more traditional sit and drink beer/piscola bars. Patio Bellavista, a large collection of upscale restaurants and bars is located here, too.

Barrio Italia

Located at the confluence of Providencia, Santiago Centro and Ñuñoa, Barrio Italia has trendy places to eat and drink. There are live music venues and a few places to dance. Prices are reasonable and there are some tourists, but mostly locals.

Moving Parties

There are parties that move locations all over the city. Some are invite only, others you can pay at the door. Look for them on Facebook and get on the list. Others are After Office, Santiago Bar Crawl, Miercoles Po, which is a party just for foreigners, plus Chilenas. I didn't really like it that much, but many of my friends did.

Other areas

Check out Ñuñoa for cheaper food and drinks and an area where hardly any foreigners go. It's fun and people are very open. Go on a Saturday and spend the afternoon walking around. Barrio Brasil is a small section in the center that has old Spanish and French style buildings and fun restaurant. It can get dicey at night so go with a Chilean. La Piojera is a classic Chilean drinking establishment, but now very touristy. Drink a terremoto or two and you'll be drunk.

CHILE: THE EXPAT'S GUIDE

SECTION 3

Culture and Sports

Chile has a fast growing cultural scene. If a band travels to South America, they'll probably be stopping Santiago. This is both good and bad. The good is that you can see world class acts on a weekly basis. The bad is that prices are outrageous by Chilean standards and similar or more expensive compared to the US . Chileans know that they'll likely only have one or two chances to see their favorite bands in their lifetime, so they're willing to spend a large portion of their income. International music festivals like Lollapallooza are popular in Chile and attract 100,000+ people over a weekend in Santiago. Santiago also attracts top international DJs on a regular basis. You can see live music in a few venues, but it's not normal to have live music in bars.

In Chile you need to search out culture more than you might in other big cities. It doesn't really have a theater, symphony, opera or orchestra culture, although the institutions do exist. The GAM is one of the most popular theaters and has plays, musicals and more. If you really need your culture fix on a world class level, go to Buenos Aires for a weekend. Chileans generally don't read much compared to the rest of the world and books are really expensive. If you like to read, bring a Kindle so you can download books for 30% of the price of a Chilean paperback. Chile has some great writers, but it seems that most Chileans don't generally take advantage of the opportunity to read them.

Soccer is the most popular sport, by far. The entire country stops when La Roja, Chile's national team, play an important game. After never winning an international trophy, Chile's national team won the Copa America twice in a row, once on home soil in 2015 and once in the US in 2016. They beat arch-rival Argentina both times.

The national league is popular, but not as popular as the European, Brazilian or Argentine leagues are in their home countries. There are three main teams: Universidad de Chile, Colo Colo and Universidad Católica. Although each team has fans from each social class, each generally appeals to a specific class: Católica, upper class, U de Chile, middle class and Colo Colo, lower class. Colo Colo has historically been the most successful team, but Universidad de Chile has been on a recent run of form, including winning the Copa Sudamericana. U de Chile and Colo Colo have the two biggest stadiums seating about 45,000.

Tickets cost between CLP$5.000 to CLP$50.000 per ticket. The areas behind the goals are reserved for the barra brava, the most rowdy fans. If you're a foreigner, I suggest avoiding these areas. Sundays games that don't feature big rivals generally have a more family atmosphere.

Estadio Nacional, Universidad de Chile's home ground, is the Chilean national team's home too. The stadium was used during the 1973 coup and ensuing dictatorship as a prison and torture center. Many people were executed and tortured there. When Chile's national team plays there, a small section is left empty in their memory and so that they can watch their national team play.

Chile has a growing movie industry and one thing I wished I'd done more of before coming to Chile, besides for practicing my Spanish, was to watch more Chilean movies to get a better sense of the country and its history. Here's a list you might be interested in checking out before you come to Chile.

Machuca – 2010, Chile. The story of a young upper class boy going to grade school during the time just before the dictatorship. Really good look into life during the early 70s in Chile. Spanish.

Missing – 1985, USA. Jack Lemon stars as an American father who comes to Chile just after the 1972 coup looking for his missing son, a Left-leaning reporter, who disappeared during the coup. Based on a true story. English.

No – 2012, Chile. The story of the 1988 referendum that let Chileans decide if they wanted to keep General Augusto Pinochet's dictatorship in power or replace it with democracy. Nominated for an Academy Award for Best Foreign Film. Spanish.

Joven y Alocada – 2011. Chile. The true story of a teenaged girl from a very religiously conservative family discovering her sexuality in high school. R rated for explicit sex. Won the prize for best script at Sundance. Spanish.

La Nana – 2009. Chile. Story about a maid, the nana, who has worked with the same upper class Chilean boss for years and their relationship. Good primer to Chilean classism. Spanish.

Que Pena tu Vida – 2010. Chile. Formulaic Chilean dating/love story movie, but worth watching after being in Chile for a few months, as you'll be able to recognize parts of Chilean culture. Spanish.

SECTION 4

Santiago Parks

Cerro San Cristobal – Cerro San Cristobal dominates the northern skyline of the city. It's a nice walk up the hill and once you get to the top you get a great view of the city and the Andes to the east. Wear a hat and sunscreen if you're going during summer or peak hours. There's also an elevator type thing if you're too lazy to walk. Entrance is at the end of Calle Pio Nono, but I like to walk down Pedro de Valdivia to the other entrance and walk up from there.

Cerro Santa Lucia – A large hill in the middle of Santiago with a cool old castle/look out point on the top. Great views of the city and shorter walk up than Cerro San Cristobal.

Cerro Santa Lucia

Parque Metropolitano – Connected to Cerro San Cristobal, I love to walk up Pedro de Valdivia to the foot of Parque Metropolitano and sit in the shade. It's a great place to get away from the noise of the city and get some work done. It's also a great place for a bbq during the weekend.

Mercado Central – Very touristy, but if you avoid the guys trying to get you to eat at their restaurants, they have an amazing selection of fresh seafood for super cheap.

Parque Bustamante – This park runs for a few miles from the Salvador metro stop all the way down town, along the river. I love walking though the park on my way to or from work.

Parque Bustamante, near Salvador metro

Plaza de Armas – The Santiago Cathedral looks like it was transplanted right out of Europe. Really cool architecture.

Plaza de Armas. Notice the police/protesters for the Obama visit.

Parque Bicentenario – Large beautiful park in Vitacura with views of the Andes, Cerro San Cristobal and the Santiago skyline.

Plaza Las Lilas – Providencia plaza/small park. Great place to relax and read during on a weekend.

Parque Forestal – Large park that winds from Baquedano to Bellas Artes along the Mapocho River.

Cajon de Maipo – Located 25-60 minutes outside of Santiago, depending on traffic it's a close oasis outside of the hustle and bustle of the city. You'll need a car o a long bus ride to get here.

Chapter 14

Banking

Chilean banks are decent, but incredibly bureaucratic and like any banks, will take advantage of you if you're not careful. You must have a RUT in order to get a bank account. I'm not sure what the banks are afraid of, but you can't get an account that allows you to deposit money and take it out in an ATM unless you have a full RUT. You'll likely need to prove that you either have an employment contract or are making over ~$700.000 per month just to open an account or over US$1,000,000 in funds ready to transfer to Chile.

Once you get a bank account, you'll need to get a multitude of documents signed, notarized and thumb printed to do seemingly basic things. And they still have bankers' hours, meaning they're only open 9am-2pm Monday to Friday. Be prepared for bureaucracy and high fees if you do anything complicated, but otherwise they aren't that bad. I have Scotiabank and didn't have any problems with them for the first two years, but they started to charge higher fees, around US$30 per month just to have a bank account. I was able to lower my fees to about US$7 per month, but it was a hassle. Banco Estado seems to be the easiest place to open an account. Look into a Cuenta RUT, which allows you all the powers of a checking account, minus being able to write checks. You can take money out via your debit card or via bank transfer, but not with checks.

Coming from the US, the coolest thing about Chilean banks is that they are all part of Transbank, a monopoly on money transfers. This means that you can instantly transfer money to any Chilean bank account right from your computer or mobile phone. It's easy, fast, free and secure. Transbank's monopoly brings up a whole host of other disadvantages, but for personal banking it's a big advantage.

Unlike in the US, if you experience credit card or bank fraud in Chile, you are responsible for the money that you lose. Be very careful with your debit and credit cards and monitor your online statements for any signs of fraud. If you plan on keeping a decent sized balance in your account, say over $2,000,000 (US$4,000), I would engage the monthly fraud protection for $2,000-$5,000 (US$4-$10), which covers any losses you suffer. I never purchase this anywhere else in the world, but in Chile, I think it's worth it.

Note: If you are a US citizen and you ever have more than US$10,000 in your account at any time, you are required to inform the IRS of its existence. Chile just agreed to auto report all of these accounts to the US as part of a recent treaty, so you really should report these accounts or risk big fines.

ATMs are very prevalent and there's no fee to withdraw using a Chilean debit card. Fees on foreign cards are generally $2,000-$3,000 (US$4-$6), so if you're using a foreign card, withdraw the max and save on fees. When withdrawing money from the ATM, the final step is to take your card out of the machine. Since most users from the US and Europe are used to getting their card back earlier in the process, it's easy to forget. Most foreigners I know have forgotten their card in a machine at least once.

If you plan to be here for a long time and don't plan on getting a RUT, you need to figure out a way to do banking without getting slammed on transaction fees. Try to get a credit card from the US or Europe that has zero international transaction fees. I have a British Airways Visa that doesn't charge transaction fees anywhere in the world. This card has saved me tons of money. Capital One also has transaction fee free cards.

Try to find a debit card that refunds your ATM transaction fees; there are some out there, so do your research before coming to Chile and find one. You'll save yourself hundreds of dollars a year. If I have my US credit card and need more money in Chile, sometimes I'll offer to pay for things for my friends with my credit card and take the cash so I can have petty cash. For an expensive lunch, that can be just as good as going to the ATM, plus I get credit card points.

Once you have permanent residence you can apply for loans from Chilean banks. You'll see offers to borrow money for consumption loans, auto loans, house loans, medical loans and more. Most of these loans have terribly high interest rates, up to 65% per year, according to Chile's consumer protection agency. Home loans aren't much higher than in the US, but the rest are borderline abusive. If you need to borrow money in Chile, be sure to shop around, rates can vary from as low as 18% up to 65%. Banks require lots of documentation, plus 3- 6 months of recent paycheck information. They likely won't lend based on assets, just on recurring income.

Chapter 15

Travel

Although you are in Chile to build your company, you are in South America and you should pull yourself away from your computer for at least a long weekend to see other parts of Chile, Argentina or Peru. Chile has some of the most beautiful and unique landscapes in the world and you'd be missing out if you don't take at least one trip. Here's some travel guides from trips my friends and I took while I've been in Chile.

Chile has two main airlines, LATAM and Sky. Both offer promotions fairly frequently, so be sure to keep an eye out. If you are flexible, check out LATAM's last minute flights. They usually have 3-4 Chilean destinations and 2-3 South American destinations for very cheap. They come out Tuesdays and run until they sell out. Be sure to search in Spanish, you'll many times find cheaper flights than in English.

SECTION 1

Pucón and the Lakes Region, Chile

My parents came to visit me in Chile at the end of April 2011 and we decided to go to Pucón and *Region de los Lagos*, the lakes region. We started off in sunny Santiago in a tiny little Chevy Spark and took the highway south. The weather was beautiful and we could still see the Andes to the east as we were driving out of the city. The route south is beautiful, starting with vineyards and wine country, later turning into rolling hills and lush greenery. A few hours south of Santiago, the sun started to set, projecting brilliant reds and pinks on the Andes.

We stopped our first night in Chillan, a medium sized town about four hours south of Santiago. We didn't see much since we were just staying over, but the town center looked really interesting. The next morning, we got up early and started to drive south again. After a few hours, we got off the main highway and drove toward a huge volcano, shrouded in clouds. I hadn't seen clouds many times since I'd been in Chile, so it was an interesting sight.

As we got closer, the weather started to get worse. We drove through Villarica and it started to drizzle. The clouds obscured the volcano. We knew it was off season and that it might be rainy in Pucón, but we had hoped it would stay dry. After a beautiful drive along the lake we got to Pucón, a small touristy town of about 25,000 people. Since it was off season, we pretty much had the place to ourselves.

People had told me that the food in the south was way better than in Santiago and I was not disappointed. The food was amazing! We started out by sharing grilled lamb and halfway through our meal, it started to pore. It was cold out and none of us had any rain gear in the restaurant, so I ran back to the car to drive it around.

One problem. The car didn't start. I had left the lights on. We tried a push start, but couldn't get it to work. I asked a police officer if he could give me a jump, he said he didn't have cables, but taxis did. I asked a colectivo, he said he didn't have any cables. I talked to four different taxis, all of whom said they couldn't help me. I even offered to pay. Finally, one taxi told me that if I bought cables he would help me. Five minutes later, I had the cables, but he had driven away. I walked back to the car, cables in hand and luckily a nice guy stopped and agreed to help out. After about an hour, we were on our way. Since the battery was dead, we had to drive around for awhile, which was alright because it was raining. This would become a recurring theme.

We stayed the night in Pucón and walked around as the clouds started to clear. We decided to take a walk on the beach. Just before sunset, it started to drizzle. Luckily, that meant we got to see a rainbow.

Later that night, we had another amazing meal. This time we split venison stew and a wild boar dish with veggies. It was hearty, warm and filling. Perfect for a cool and rainy night. The next morning, it was raining again and we planned to take a drive toward Argentina, but when I tried to start the car, it was dead. The guy at the hotel jumped us and we decided to drive around to other towns to charge it up again. The weather started to clear in the afternoon and we drove through a bunch of small towns and ended up in Villarica, a less touristy town 20 miles from Pucón. We stayed above an Italian restaurant, walked around the city and ate some great fish at a small restaurant.

The next morning, the car started up like a charm and we took a drive toward the Argentina border. We drove through a bunch of small towns and were pretty much the only tourists. Each town was a little different and the weather was perfect. Curarrehue was a hidden gem. We walked around, checked out the Mapuche museum and then walked into a bakery on the main plaza for a small snack. We smelled something amazing and I asked what it was. The baker, Elisa, brought out fresh baked meat empanadas and we decided we had to have some. They were amazing, the best I've had in Chile. After we finished, she came out with the fried version. Amazing again.

Next, we tried some bakery and check out some local canned fruits and jams. Everything was wild picked, nothing was farmed. After a few minutes, she emerged from the kitchen with some amazing berry spread. The baker had been invited to London and Dublin a few years back to make all of her food at the embassy and I can see why they picked her.

After we finished, we got back to the car and what do you know? Another dead battery. I asked a guy at the only gas station in town and he said he couldn't help me, but there was a mechanic just down the street. As I walked up, all the workers and truckers stopped and just sort of stared. I don't think they were expecting a family of tourists. The mechanic was out to lunch, so I went back up to the gas station and sat there until someone agreed to give me a jump again. Thankfully, this was the last time we'd need our jumper cables.

We drove through the beautiful mountain valleys, past crystal clear lakes and shaded passes under the bright sunlight. We came to little town called Huife and decided to turn around. As we were driving back, I saw a sign for a restaurant that was advertising fresh trout, turkey and venison, so we had to stop. We were the only people around, besides the waitress/cook and the food was amazing. Rich, savory and fresh. It was a great decision to stop.

We stayed another night in Pucón and the next day, the weather was really nice and went up the volcano. It is a huge volcano that has a history of erupting, sometimes destroying the surrounding towns. It was cloudy in Pucón, but we emerged from the clouds into bright sunlight about halfway up the volcano. The clouds looked like icing on a cake, covering the valley. We took a hike up the volcano and started when it was bright and sunny. It was amazing to see the evidence of past lava flows and the destruction it wreaked on the vegetation. About an hour later, the pea soup had descended and we couldn't see more than a few feet in front of our faces. Luckily, the trail was very well marked. The fog was eerie and outlined the trees perfectly.

The next morning, we drove back to Santiago, capping a great trip to the south. Although the weather and car trouble were less than optimal, it was an outstanding trip. I'm really glad my parents got a chance to visit and got to spend some time sharing where I'd been living for the past six months. I really loved the area around Pucón. The combination of lakes, mountains, lush green scenery and amazing food is pretty hard to beat.

Section 2

Valparaiso, Viña del Mar, Reñaca, Maitencillo, Cachagua, Zapallar Chile

Valparaíso was an incredibly important port in South America as the first stop for ships after going around the southern tip of the continent. It was rich, full of culture and interesting architecture. That all changed when the Panama Canal opened. Shipping dried up and Valpo stopped growing. Today, it still has many of the charms of the old city and you can walk around the city's many big hills. Parts are dangerous and run down, while others are completely safe and beautiful. Named a UNESCO World Heritage Site, it offers top restaurants, bohemian arts and interesting old architecture.

Viña del Mar is much smaller and about a 10 minute drive from Valpo. It's touristy and a place where people go to escape the heat in the summer. There are two beaches, one in Viña and another a few minutes drive up the coast, in Reñaca.

As you go north, you'll go through Con Con and other small beach enclaves. They get more upscale as you go north, with Maitencillo, Cachagua and Zapallar about an hour or two drive to the north. They are nice places to get away for the weekend when you're tired of the city. You can travel to all of them via bus that leaves from central Santiago.

SECTION 3

Torres del Paine, Chile

My brother Jake came to visit in May 2011 and we decided to go south to Patagonia since he loves hiking. My friend Tiago Matos, another Startup Chile entrepreneur, came along and we had a great time exploring the amazing beauty of the Magallanes Province.

We took a 3.5 hour flight south to Punta Arenas and then a 4 hour bus to Puerto Natales. Since we had some no planning and it was the low season, we needed up having to rent a jeep instead of taking the buses. We stayed over in Puerto Natales then set out really early to get to the park. We drove in on a wet, gray day and went past deep blue water and glacier carved landscapes. We arrived at the edge of Lago Pehoé and took the catamaran across the incredibly smooth water. The weather was warm, but rainy and the water was an amazing shade of light blue.

We arrived to the other side and checked into a refugio. It was super nice, but seemed to be expensive, about $50 per night for a bed, but the location was unreal. We walked down the path, through the rain down toward Glacier Grey. Jake and I had to turn around, as it was getting dark, so we didn't get a close up look at the glacier, but the walk was beautiful. We got back and ate dinner in the warm lodge.

We slept in the next day and woke up to amazing weather. It was a little cooler, but sunny and clear. We took the ferry across the lake, got back in the jeep and drove across crappy roads toward the base of Torres del Paine. The water was unlike any other color I've seen, except maybe in the Swiss Alps.

We set off up the path at about 215pm with the goal of walking about 1.5 hours, dropping off our bags at the refugio and then going another 2.5 hours to the top, then back 2 hours down. After one hour, we realized that the refugio was closed for winter and that if we wanted to see the top, we'd have to go all the way up and down before about 8pm when it got dark. A slight hitch in the plan, so we booked it and did a fast pace up and back down. We knew we'd cut it close, but it was our last day so we were willing to push it.

The walk was beautiful. A combo of the Pacific Northwest and the Great Smokey Mountains, but bigger and more colorful. It was fall, so the trees were red, orange and green. We crossed glacial mountain streams on small wooden bridges and went up and down the small hills through the forest. We were moving fast and with our packs, so it was pretty tiring. The last hour was 300 meters up in about 1km. It was super steep. After struggling for a bit, I had to take my pack off and walk to the top.

We got to the top and saw the Torres with a small glacier lake below. It was a little cloudy, so we didn't see all of it at once, but it was completely worth it. It was amazing to hear the water rushing down the mountain sides directly from the melting glaciers. We hustled back down the valley as the light was beginning to fade. We had to make sure we were mostly out off the trail by the time it got dark since we didn't have any big lights with us. The sun was setting over the valley and we were getting close to the bottom. The moon rose and the stars were beautiful as we walked the last 20 minutes in the dark. My body ached from the pace, the pack and generally being used to living in the city.

Patagonia is a beautiful special place. I wish I had more time to explore and I would love to come back some day and see the rest of the park, Calafate, Bariloche and the rest of Chilean and Argentine Patagonia. We drove back to Natales and ate a lamb grill while waiting for the bus. The town is basically base camp with tons of coffee shops, restaurants and places to buy/ rent gear. It was a cool town, but we didn't get to see much. It was a quick trip to Patagonia, about as short as we could do it. I really enjoyed going out of season, as the weather was perfect for hiking and there were hardly any people. It would have been nice to do a full 5-6 days, but with 3 days actually in the park, it was definitely worth it. One of the most beautiful places I've ever been to.

Section 4

San Pedro de Atacama, Chile

I spent four days in and around San Pedro de Atacama, in the far north of Chile, about two hours north of Santiago by flight. Atacama is one of the strangest, most beautiful, rugged, remote, stunning places I've ever been. Normally, I really dislike tours and prefer to go out on my own, but San Pedro is the exception. I went with a friend's business called Pathway Chile which takes mostly young people on trips around Chile. I paid about US$400 for four days of hostel, flight, day trips and a few meals. Our group consisted of 12 people from six different countries and was really fun.

I think it would be extremely hard to do San Pedro on your own because of the terrain, weather and impossibility to get around. Over our four days, our guides drove rugged buses and 4x4s over mountains, volcanoes, salt flats, desserts and much more. The network of mostly dirt roads can be deadly for even the most experienced drivers who know the area. The roads were lined with little shrines to mark previous accidents.

San Pedro the town is a bit strange. It's in the middle of nowhere, with the closest airport about 1.5 hours away in Calama. It's made up of restaurants, hostels, bars and tchotchke shops. It's a tourist trap, but the scenery more than makes up for it.

I saw more weird/stunning things in four days that I think I've seen anywhere else in the world. Our first day, we went for a drive to Valle de la Luna, aptly named because it looks like the surface of the moon. We played around on huge sand dunes and sprinted down to get to the bottom. Liberating. People were sand boarding, which looked cool, but I bet hurt a lot.

We went to the amphitheater to watch the sun set, which was absolutely unreal. The sky was on fire. It was truly the best sunset I've ever seen, even better than Cape Town. We hiked through a cavern and looked at the star filled night sky while the moon came up in the sky. The night sky in Northern Chile is the best in the world and there are international telescopes all over the place.

The second day, we went for a drive through small towns and ended up at two lakes at the foot of a perfectly conical volcano. It was beautiful. There were lots of flamingos, which are pink because of the creatures they eat. They eliminate the beta carotene via their feathers, hence the pink. The redder the flamingo, the older (or fatter) he is. We ate lunch at a tiny town of about 100 people where they grew all of the food in a garden out back.

Lunch was quinoa, rice, bean soup, followed by potato, bean and quinoa main dish. It was hearty, spicy and good. that night we ended up at a flamingo sanctuary, where we saw our second amazing sunset in a row. It reflected off the water and outlined the flamingos against the backdrop of the mountains.

We got up at 330am the next day to find it raining. We took a 2 hour ride up to about 4500m to see hot springs and geysers. The mountains had a fresh coat of snow, which almost never happens. We ate breakfast high above the geyser field under the cover of the snow capped mountains. We hung out in the hot springs to warm up. Before we left, we check out the active mud vents and sulfur vents. Since we were so high up, it was a bit hard to breathe if we did any sort of extended exercise.

In the afternoon, we went to the eyes of the desert, which are two random holes in the middle of the desert believed to be caused by meteor strikes. These two perfectly circular holes are about 40 meters across and super deep and filled with water. We jumped from about 20 feet up into the refreshing, salty water.

Next, we went to Laguna Cejar, the saltiest lake in the world, even more than the Dead Sea. We floated around and enjoyed the sun. You can't even go under water if you try and it was comical to see people try. When we got out, we had to get hosed down because there was so much salt on us.

We ended the day at salt flats to watch the sun set. It was a great scene with the mountains in the background. The salt flats had a bit of water on them, so they reflected everything. Luckily they were only a preview to the salt flats of Uyuni. On our last day, we went for a drive up to the Bolivian border and through the mountains. The weather was amazing. Rain, snow, hail, sun, lightning in a short period of time. We saw an amazing red sunset, capped off by more flamingos and Vincuñas, which are sort of like llamas. The beauty and force of nature was humbling and reminded me how lucky we really are. I've never seen colors and such quick changing weather like that.

That night, we packed up to head out to Bolivia the next morning. It was an incredibly interesting trip and not very expensive. If you're going to San Pedro, I recommend 3-4 days, it's worth it.

SECTION 5

Pichilemu, Chile

Pichilemu is a small surfing town about four hours south of Santiago by bus. A few Start-Up Chile friends and I went to this beautiful surf town in 2011, right when we were getting settled in Chile. It was just the break I needed from the heat of Santiago in the middle of the summer. There were huge beaches, big waves, warm sun, great food and interesting people.

We stayed at an awesome hostel, right on the beach, about five minutes walk from the town center called Pichilemu Surf Hostel. The owner is a Dutch guy who bought the land about 20 years ago for $12,000 and built the hostel himself. He had to completely rebuild in the last year after a tsunami wiped out his beach front property after the huge earth quake from a year ago. Many buildings were damaged in Pichilemu and a few were killed, including a few tourists. We saw the evidence on a beach where the only thing that remained of beach front restaurants was the floor.

The seafood was phenomenal and cheap. Fisherman hauled their catch in and came right up onto the beach to sell their catch. They were selling 3 whole fish, cleaned and filleted for $2. They has fresh shrimp, crab, barnacles, conger eel and even a little shark. We stopped for a super fresh white fish ceviche on the beach for about $2 and later that night shared a pastel de jaiba, which is sort of like a crab/cheese casserole. I had fried conger eel, which is really a white fish that tastes sort of like cod. It was truly awesome food.

We watched the sun set over the pacific each day and then drank cheap beer and wine either by a fire or at one of the local bars. We met new friends at bars and everyone went to the beach to drink, play music and have fun until 7am. It was my kind of town and I wish I could have stayed for longer. If you like to cook and go to Pichilemu, rent a cheap cabin with a kitchen and take advantage of the amazing seafood!

SECTION 6

La Serena & Valle Del Elqui, Chile

My friends Forrest and Sarah came to visit all the way from Wisconsin, so my Entrustet business partner Jesse, Forrest, Sarah and I decided to take a trip north to La Serena and Valle del Elqui. La Serena is a town of 150,000 about 4.5 hours north of Santiago. Along with it's sister city of Coquimbo, it's located on miles of wide, white sand beaches. It reminded me of Panama City Beach, FL but not during spring break.

We stayed at an apartment on the beach that we found on AirBnB. Yanette, the owner, was extremely nice. She's been living in La Serena for about 25 years and also owns a wine producing property northeast of the coast. She brought us amazing grapes and raisins as a thank you for renting that were truly the best I've ever had. They were sweet, plump and way better than you can get in the US. The grapes we get less sweet, because they have to harvest them earlier to ship them to the US.

The drive up is on a four lane highway, mostly along the coast. It reminds me a bit of highway 1 in California, with lots of hills, twists and turns. The small towns all have goat cheese sandwiches and fruit stands along the highways, while we only have McDonalds and Taco Bell in the US. So much better here. I wish I had rented a little bit better car because it would have been great to go up the hills and around the bends in a real car.

Our first day, we walked down the beach and got lunch at a small restaurant. For $7, we got a seafood empanada FULL of every kind of seafood you could think of. Next, a seafood soup filled with oysters in a spicy cilantro broth. The main course was fried reinata with sweet tomatoes and then dessert was super ripe honeydew melon. Great value and great food.

Next, we went over to the Coquimbo fist market and bought mussels, scallops and a full dorada. The fisherman cut it up into huge filets so we could cook them on the stove top. We also got an assortment of fruit and veggies from a little stand and came back to the beach apartment to cook.

We created an amazing meal. We started with a seafood soup with dorada, assorted seafood, ají, potato, carrots and other veggies. Next, pineapple and pepper ceviche with mussels, scallops and dorada. It was great. The main course was dorada a la plancha with a salt/curry rub, curried veggies and a pineapple salsa. Dessert was vanilla ice cream with a sweet grape and white wine sauce. It was a great way to end the day.

The next day we tried to go to Punta de Chorros to sea an island full of penguins. After a beautiful 2 hour drive through the mountains and across a few dirt roads, our little car finally stopped at a restaurant where we had some fresh fish. The highlight was their home made olive oil, infused with garlic and hot peppers. We each ended up buying a half liter bottle for about $7 to take home. Amazing. Unfortunately, when we got to the fishing dock, the fishermen told us that they couldn't take us because the sea was too choppy. I think he was just being lazy and didn't only want to take a group of 4, but it was still a great day. We watched the waves crash on the rugged Pacific coast and then made the drive back to La Serena.

The next morning, we left early and headed into Valle del Elqui. It started out cloudy, but it soon burned off to reveal a narrow valley filled with fruit trees, pisco distilleries and vineyards. Every Chilean I had talked to had told me that I had to go to Valle del Elqui if I was going near La Serena and they were 100% right. It was beautiful.

We stopped in Vicuña, the birthplace of Gabriela Mistral and strolled around their town square. We ate lunch while listening to music in the town square and then had some fresh pecans and homemade ice cream from a little shop on the square. We continued onward and finally stopped in Pisco Elqui, the hear of Chile's pisco growing region. We toured the Mistral pisco distillery and got to see the whole process. The tasting was interesting. The really aged pisco tasted almost like a whiskey and was supposed to be served over ice or alone. I'm used to piscola, so it was quite different. After, we continued down the curvy road to Alcohuaz, doing the last 15k on a tiny dirt road. It was a beautiful drive, ending at an eco lodge called Casona Distante.

This place is amazing. It's in the middle of nowhere, no cell reception and is beautiful. It's on 40 acres of land in the middle of the valley and is a functioning grape growing operation. They sell their grapes to Capel to make pisco and still raise animals and other fruit. The lodge is built mostly of wood and the rooms are beautiful. They have an open kitchen where you can watch or help prepare dinner and our chef Alejandro was awesome. We got lessons on Chilean cooking and drink making and talked about food, politics and Chile. His palta (avocado) sour was amazing, especially after adding some aji.

Casona Distante also has a nice observatory and the owner helped us look at nebulae and Saturn. You really can see it's rings! Looking up into the sky and seeing millions of stars is amazing. The night sky there was only bested by my trip to Bolivia, as we were about 2500 meters higher, so the sky was clearer. The next day, we hung around the lodge and checked out the river that runs through the valley. It was relaxing and beautiful, but unfortunately, we had to go back to Santiago at the end of the day. I would have loved to stay longer, but it wasn't possible. I highly recommend going to Valle del Elqui for a long weekend, it was one of my favorite places I've been so far.

Section 7

Buenos Aires, Argentina

Buenos Aires is my favorite city in South America and up there with my favorite cities in the world. Although Buenos Aires proper has a population of 4m, it's really a huge city of 12m along Mar de La Plata, where the River Plata empties into the sea. Most people in the US assume that since Chile and Argentina share such a long border and are in South America that they have a lot in common. But they're really different: the accents, clothes, personalities and culture. In reality the two things they have in common are Spanish and a love of asados.

Buenos Aires is a city of amazing food, good looking people, beautiful architecture, wine, beef, culture, nightlife and fashion. It's the Paris of South America, but with a South American edgy flair. People are generally educated, thanks to good public education and free universities, and love to socialize. Economically, it's the Italy of South America: fiscal problems, a left wing government that's nationalized industries and imposed currency controls to try to dedollarize the economy, which has led to rampant inflation and a black market exchange rate. When I first traveled to Buenos Aires in November 2011, the market rate was 4.2 pesos to a dollar and 4.5 to a dollar on the street. One year later it was 4.5:1 officially and 7.5:1 on the street.

People like their leisure time. There's huge public and private sector unions with massive clout and lots of strikes. While I've been in Buenos Aires there have been strikes by truckers, airport baggage handlers and garbage collectors. There's tons of red tape and bureaucracy and its no coincidence that Spanish speaking LatAm's biggest entrepreneurial successes have come from Argentina: you learn from a young age how to be entrepreneurial and get things done by bending and breaking the rules. As it stands now, I wouldn't do business in Argentina, but it is my favorite place to visit.

Argentina has the best food of anywhere I've been in Latin America and quite possibly the world. While I've had my best meal in Latin America in Mendoza, some of the next best have been in Buenos Aires. And it's not just at the top end. Buenos Aires is a city where people love and appreciate food. You can walk into just about any little cafe, bakery or restaurant and expect a good meal.

Buenos Aires is know for two things: steak and Italian food, but it's much more than that. But first, lets start with the steak. Argentina has some of the best beef in the world, most of which is produced by cows that eat grass, walking around on ranches in La Pampa, Argentina's livestock belt. The most popular cut is the Bife Chorizo, which is certainly not any kind of sausage. It's most closely related to a sirloin or NY Strip steak in the US. It's my favorite. They're also famous for their Malbec, which mostly comes from Mendoza in the north.

We went to La Cabrera, a touristy steak place in Palermo, at about 1030 for dinner. It's expensive for Argentina, but it was worth it. The 600 gram steak, paired with a full bodied Malbec, was incredible. They gave us free drinks at the end of the meal because they didn't have a dessert drink I asked about. Buenos Aires has some of the best restaurant service in the world because waiters were a profession up until recently. There's still guys who have been waiting tables for decades who know everything there is to know about food, wine and service. It's such a contrast to Chile and many restaurants in the US.

After we finished eating at 1230, we headed out to have a drink. We found a bar filled with interesting people, cheap drinks and interesting decor. After a few Quilmes it was 3am and we decided to go actually go out. We found a club with a line and walked it. Like in Chile people eat and go out late, but Argentina is even later. The place was just getting started.

We closed the place at 630 and found our way back to the apartment we rented on Airbnb

Argentina has some of, if not the best, gelato in the world and we couldn't resist grabbing a scoop for breakfast as we walked from Palermo to Recoleta to check out the cemetery where Buenos Aires' elite are buried. It's a labyrinth of extremely decorated mausoleums right in the middle of the city. Its amazing to see how much people spent on a cemetery that occupies prime land! After the cemetery, we stopped for a quick sandwich at La Biela under the shade of one of the more interesting trees I've ever seen.

After a quick bite, we wandered around Recoleta, taking in the embassies, old mansions and high end shops on our way down toward Av 9 de Julio, the world's wides boulevard at 14 lanes. As we walked down toward the obelisk, Teatro Colon and finally Casa Rosada, the presidential palace. The city just oozes history and architectural brilliance. Buenos Aires was on par with London at one point in the 1800s and they used the wealth to build incredible buildings and one of the oldest subways in the world. Unlike London, Buenos Aires hasn't done much to update the metro, which we took back for the night. We had dinner at Broccolino, an Italian place with incredible lamb raviolis.

The next day, we took the Subte (subway), down toward La Boca, the area of the city known for the colored houses and of course the soccer team. The walk from the metro station took us through a few rougher areas, but it was great to see the difference in parts of the city. The entire area is dominated by the imposing La Bombonera, where Boca play their matches. When finally we got to the port, it was super touristy with guys trying to steer us into their bars. We left after some beers and empanadas.

We headed back up toward San Telmo and since it was Sunday we wandered across the famous street market where you'll find just about everything for sale. We had a late lunch at a small Italian restaurant and walked around the old cobblestone streets. As it got darker and the traffic went away, you could almost feel yourself going back in time. We stopped into a small dive bar full of immigrants from eastern Europe for a cheap drink and hung out for awhile taking in the scene, then headed back up toward Palermo to meet some friends.

Our friends decided they wanted to go out in Puerto Madero, the newly developed area of town along the river, which had sat vacant and underdeveloped for decades. Now its revitalized with glitzy clubs, top restaurants and interesting people. It's expensive compared to the rest of the city, but we had a good time. It wasn't really my favorite place because it just doesn't feel much different from any other big city in the world, maybe because its so new, but my friends and the many other tourists who were there loved it.

The next day we decided to walk to el Ateno, an old theater that's been converted into a bookstore. The inside is beautifully converted and it was packed with tourists and locals alike. We stopped for another ice cream and took it all in. We took a taxi back to Palermo and decided to do some shopping. Palermo has many boutiques and you can watch as Argentines and tourists alike shop for fashionable clothes. Although the sticker prices are high, typically $75-$150 for a button down shirt, if you're exchanging dollars that you brought with you, you can save up to 60%. One store owner heard me speaking in my accented Spanish and asked if I had dollars to spend and quoted me a 50% discount. After our shopping, it was off to the airport. Luckily we'd booked for Aeroparque, which is in the city, instead of Ezezia, which is a $40, hour long drive outside of the city.

There's so many more amazing places I missed in this post that you'll have to discover for yourself. Buenos Aires is an incredible city that should be on your list of places to visit if you have the chance. And right now it's a great value and likely will keep getting better as their economy continues to have problems. I can't wait to go back again.

SECTION 8

Mendoza, Argentina

About 120 miles and one huge mountain range separate Santiago and Mendoza, Argentina. Instead of a 2 hour drive, it's an 8-12 hour drive through the Andes Mountains. (Tips on how to drive to Mendoza at the end of this section). You can go by plane in about 40 minutes. Mendoza had been on our list of places to visit and when Mendoza showed up LAN Airlines' Last Minute specials for about $70, we decided to book a weekend. If you're traveling in South America, make sure to look at the prices in Spanish, they were 50% cheaper than the ones in English.

Mendoza is a laid back city of Malbec, beef & pasta, olive oil, ice cream and beautiful, wide streets, set at the foot of the Andes mountains. A little over 100k people live in Mendoza proper, but the city sprawls out to include about 850k people in the suburbs and surrounding area. Central Mendoza sort of reminded me of an Argentine Madison in terms of size and pace of life. The city is set out in a grid system emanating from the beautiful, green Plaza de Independencia in the middle. Main streets are wide boulevards with ample pedestrian walkways shaded by large trees. The streets are lined with cafes, restaurants and gelato parlors.

Mendoza is much cheaper than Santiago and clearly less developed. The houses and buildings look a bit older, but it's still a very well developed city. Argentina has a large Italian influence, so that means pasta and gelato, along with a more sing-songy Spanish. They also pronounce words that have the "LL" as more of a "sh", although less so than in Buenos Aires. They often say "vos" instead of "tú" and speak slower and more clearly than most Chileans. There also seems to be a higher penetration of English, but that could be because we were in a touristy part of the city and Mendoza is a touristy city.

Nightlife starts even later in Mendoza. We ate dinner at about 10pm and we were pretty much the only people in the restaurant. It filled up by about 1045. We went out to for some drinks about 12/1 and the clubs weren't even open yet. They start to open at 2am and then close around 6/7am. Mendozans take a siesta, which means just about everything is close for an hour or two in the afternoon. Everything and I mean everything was closed on Sunday.

On Friday, we took the short flight over the Andes and checked into our hostel. It was about $15 per person per night and located close to the city center. We walked around for a few hours, ate some great gelato and then met some friends for lunch on one of Mendoza's many wide boulevards. We walked to a nice park and then went back to the hostel for a bit of a rest. After awhile, we checked out The Vines of Mendoza, which was started by two guys fro Austin, TX. They had a great selection local wines and you could get a great class for about $2-3. They also had a great cheese and meat plate with some great blue cheese.

Next, we went out for dinner at an Italian restaurant named La Marchigiania that the taxi driver recommended. We shared an amazing caprese salad that included the best balsamic vinegar I've ever had. Next, we split two different types of steak and a spinach and pasta dish that were both top notch. Dessert was a chocolate fudge ball, covered in ice cream, then covered in hard chocolate. By about 12:30am, we had our fill and asked for the bill. For two appetizers, four main courses, three nice bottles of wine and a dessert, our bill came out to about $75 total, or about $19 each, including tip. Needless to say, we were impressed by the quality and price of Argentine food.

The next day, we got up early and went on a wine tour. The four of us booked a driver and three wineries and spent the day in the beautiful wine country at the foot of the Andes. Our first winery was Cavas de Don

Arturo, a small family owned winery that only produces a small amount of wine by hand each year. We tried a few different wines and took at tour of the beautiful winery. Next we went to Septima, which is part of a large Spanish company. It was quite the contrast between a small, handmade winery and a large, commercial operation.

We ended our tour at Ruca Mallen, where we booked lunch. For $50, we had a six course tasting menu, with six wine pairings. The Ruca Mallen outdoor dining area is an amazing place to eat and the meal matched the setting. The highlights were the quinoa lemon & olive oil salad, pumpkin milanesa and the fig crusted steak. All of the food was great. The best wine of the day was a 2002 Cabernet Sauvignon and Malbec blend that was paired with the steak. This $50 meal would have cost $175-200 in the US and the wine alone was probably $75-100 in the US, maybe more. The value for money was top notch.

That night, we slept off our meal and then checked out some of the nightlife. It was nice and relaxing and after the huge meal and wine, we ended up calling it a night fairly early by Mendoza standards. The next day, we woke up and took a minibus about 45 minutes outside of the city into a canyon with a river flowing through it. There was a public pool which reminded me of a smaller Wisconsin Dells and an upscale spa that was really expensive, so we just joined the other locals and walked down into the canyon and hung out by the river. We had lunch at a small asado restaurant and ate costillar (beef ribs) that had been grilled with real wood about thirty yards away. We spent the rest of the day lounging around and then took the minibus back to the hostel.

We decided to have one more top notch meal and ended up at 1884 for another top notch meal. I had another steak and we all shared appetizers and wine. The highlight was a goat cheese and apple salad with an interesting balsamic. The outdoor setting was beautiful, the food was great and the conversation was even better. While good, I thought the other two meals we had were better values. Although we can't spend any Startup Chile money on our travels, the weekend was an expense I was willing to pay. We all needed a relaxing break away from Santiago and our businesses.

TRAVELOGUE: DRIVING FROM SANTIAGO, CHILE TO MENDOZA, ARGENTINA

My parents came to visit last week and we decided to rent a car and drive over the Andes to visit Mendoza for Vendimia, the grape harvest festival. I've already been to Mendoza , but I'd never driven over the Andes, which is always rated one of the best drives in South America.

For someone used to flying into countries or driving between the US and Canada, there are a surprising amount of hoops you have to jump through before you're even able to go from Chile to Argentina, especially if you're renting a car. First, you must have a notarized letter of permission from the car owner that says you're legally able to take the car out of Chile. Next you have to have a special type of insurance for the entire time you're in Argentina or else Chile won't let you out and Argentina won't let you in. You also have to carry proof of insurance with you at all times, especially at the border. If your insurance is expired when you try to come back to Chile, Argentina reserve the right to keep the car until you personally come back with valid insurance. Lastly, you have to have the customs form that lists when the car has gone out/in of Chile in the past.

If you don't have ALL of them, you won't be able to leave and will have to turn around at the border. Make sure you call to reserve your rental car a few days ahead of time, as the agencies need time to get the paperwork in order. Most companies ask for a week in advance, but I was able to do it with two days notice. My insurance and all of the paperwork cost CLP$70.000 (US$140) for five days in Argentina and I probably could have gotten it a little cheaper if I had shopped around.

Once I took care of all of that, we got on the road. We left Santiago and headed northwest into the foothills toward the city of Los Andes. The first hour or so is on nice four lane highway, but as you make your way toward Portillo, the sky center, it turns into a winding two lain highway with some significant drop-offs. It can be frustrating because trucks have to travel incredibly slowly and there aren't many passing zones.

There's currently construction on the Chilean side of the border to make the road safer and the countries have agreed alternate traffic. You can go into Argentina from 20:00 to 07:00 and back into Chile from 08:00 to 19:00. This construction is likely to go on for at least another two months.

We arrived at the construction zone at about 18:30 and had to wait until about 20:30 to get moving. There were probably 60 cars ahead of us, plus another 100 behind us by the time we got moving. It ended up being a mess because everyone arrived at the border crossing at the same time. When there's no construction, you can arrive at any time cross. Total driving time should be around 5 hours. In our case, it took us 7 hours of driving time because we had to wait in a huge line at the border.

Because of the construction we had to cross at night, so we didn't get a feeling of just how big the mountains were on the way into Argentina. But I felt myself steadily driving up on nice wide two lane highways. All of the sudden we reached a sign that said "zona de curvas peligrosas" dangerous curves, and we started to go up, straight up. It was mesmerizing watching the cars zigzagging up the hairpin turns, seeing the white and red lights like tiny ants on the mountain above us. There were 28 curves in all and it took us almost 45 minutes to cover the 7km to the top.

The border crossing is located at the top, just before the Cristo Redentador tunnel that connects Chile and Argentina. The countries have partnered together to have a shared border control all in one place. There's four steps: first, show your auto papers, insurance, permission to leave Chile, etc, that we talked about before. If you don't have it, Chile won't let you out of the country and will send you back down the mountain. Second, you have to have the correct papers to leave Chile, your passport or identity card. After those papers are stamped, you move onto Argentinian border control. The Argentinians stamp your passports and check to make sure you have your insurance paid up and that the Chileans have let you take your car out of the country. Another stamp.

If you're from the US, Canada or Australia, you must pay the reciprocity fee ahead of time and bring the printout. The rules just changed in February and they don't have anyone at the border to take your money. They were nice enough to let us use their personal computer to pay the fee and print out the paper, or they would have sent us back down the mountain and into Chile. Previously, Argentina only collected this fee if you flew into Ezeiza airport in Buenos Aires.

Next, you pass to Argentinian customs where they make sure you're not bringing in contraband or huge amounts of dollars. Since we were clearly tourists, they just asked two questions and let us go. All told, we were at the border for about two and a half hours. On the return trip, it only took us 30 minutes.

The road down from the border slowly slopes down, following the path of a large river. After about an hour, you arrive at Upsallata, a small resort town in a beautiful valley. From there's it's another hour and a half, at least to Mendoza. Make sure to watch out for trucks. We saw three different trucks completely flipped over and could smell burning breaks on countless others. They drive about 20km per hour going down the mountain, making for interesting passing in no passing zone opportunities.

After three days in Mendoza, we drove back to Chile during daylight. The mountains are huge and colors change quickly as you drive farther in. We stopped at Upsallata for a bbq lunch at a truck stop, which was one of the better lunches I've had. The owners were preparing their own Sunday family lunch and served us some of what they were going to eat: five cuts of beef, two types of sausage, potatoes, a tomato, onion and lettuce salad and homemade bread. It was just what I needed to make the drive up over the mountains and back into Chile.

The drive itself lived up to its billing. It's a beautiful, fun drive, but make sure you have all of your paperwork in order or you might get turned around at the border. I wouldn't want to try it in winter though!

SᴇᴄᴛɪᴏN 9

Uyuni, Bolivia

I've taken the overland trip from San Pedro de Atacama to Salar de Uyuni twice, once in 2011 and once in 2014. I've included both of my reactions to both of my trips so you can get an idea of how things have changed and how each trip is very different.

UYUNI 2010

I took four days to explore southwestern Bolivia. Bolivia is the poorest country in all of Latin America and it shows. I didn't see a single paved road, even the roads in Uyuni that connect the city of 20,000 with both of the two capitals. Although it's very poor, it seemed very safe. The overwhelmingly indigenous population seemed laid back and welcoming. The Bolivian president Evo Morales claims to be the first indigenous president of a South American country and his picture was everywhere.

Bolivia is poor in large part to losing a huge swathe of land, including its access to the sea, to Chile in a war in the 1880s. They also lost huge mineral deposits in the mineral rich northern part of what is now Chile. There is still huge animosity between Chile, Bolivia and Peru, much of it stemming from this war in the 1880s.

Our four day trek took us through amazing terrain, culminating in the Salar de Uyuni, which is the worlds largest salt flat. I went with five people from the San Pedro trip and we booked our trip in city center a few days before we wanted to leave. Our package cost $180 and included all transportation, three nights accommodation, four days of meals and a tour guide. US Citizens have to pay $140 to enter most South American countries because we slapped a fee on South American citizens after 9/11 (really dumb), but I got away with only paying a portion of the fee at the tiny border crossing with some well placed...words.

We entered Bolivia and were immediately in the Eduardo Avaroa national park, a joint venture between the Bolivia government and the European Union. We drove past laguna blanca, a perfectly clear lake that reflects the sky. It was a beautiful and a great start to the trip. We drove across bumpy dirt roads, sometimes covered with water from the melting snow on the mountains. Our guide told us he had never seen snow on the mountains in February in his three years of guiding, so again, we were incredibly lucky. The mountains and stark landscape were stunning.

Next, we got to a hot springs at the foot of a mountain lake. We were at 4800m, which meant that there was only about 44% as much oxygen compared to sea level. It made breathing difficult and we all got light headed after 20 minutes in the hot springs. the lake was full of colors and we could see lightning over the tops of mountains far in the distance.

After another few hour drive, we got to Laguna Colorada, which has blood red water. We ate homemade soup and fresh veggies for lunch, prepared by our guide. After lunch, we took a walk to an overlook point and watched the flamingos and the scenery. It was incredibly windy and I was glad that I bought a wool sweater the day before.

My head hurt from the altitude, so I tried chewing some coca leaves, which is supposed to relieve your headache. You mash 6-10 leaves in between your lip and your gum and let it sit there. You can add bicarbonate and it releases more of the drug. 30 minutes later, I felt a little like I had ADD, but my headache was gone. We also tried coca tea, which sort of tasted like seaweed in sushi restaurants. Both clearly helped.

We spent the night at the hostel overlooking Laguna Colorada. The night sky was absolutely stunning, even better than San Pedro. The stars twinkled and I think I could see more stars that I've ever seen anywhere else in the world. The combination of the altitude and lack of light pollution showed how truly small we are. A shooting star topped it off and told me it was time to go to bed.

The hostel was cold, but my sleeping bag kept me war. We had been warned not to drink alcohol or eat meat, but I had a very small glass of wine, maybe 2 oz, with dinner and woke up with a splitting headache. The thin air makes alcohol really hard on your body. The bathroom was really bad, so I just went outside when I had to go.

The next morning, we drove across the Bolivian altiplano, stopping at strange, beautiful scenery every few minutes. We ate a snack at a string of lagoons that reflected the mountains perfectly and continued past land-marks that looked like Dali paintings. That afternoon we dined on llama, eggs, veggie soup in a town of 150 in the middle of nowhere. The food was fantastic, balanced and healthy. The eggs were from chickens running around the parking lot outside and tasted different than the factory eggs we get in the States.

We ended the day in Uyuni, a town of 20,000 near the Salar. We ate dinner in a massive thunder storm. I didn't have a raincoat, so I used a trash bag, which an 8 year old Chilean on the trip thought was hilarious. I told him it was the new fashion, straight from Santiago, and he couldn't stop laughing. The hotel was nice, with flushing toilets and a shower. We had time to check out the town, which is bustling with energy. It had rained, so there was water in some parts of the dirt roads.

Kids were having tons of fun with squirt guns and water balloons, throwing them at their friends (and random people) of the opposite sex. I got crushed twice by 6-10 year old girls yelling "get the gringo" as they were laughing and playing. I was really tempted to buy a squirt gun and join the battles, but we didn't have time.

We went to bed early sot hat we could get to the salar the next day. We first stopped at a cemetery for trains, which has a bunch of 80-100 year old trains that used to run between Chile, Bolivia and Argentina. They were cool looking and full of history and our guide told us there are plans to build a proper museum. After a bit, we finally got to the salar.

The salar is a huge salt flat that sometimes is covered by 1-3 inches of water. We were extremely lucky to visit while it was flooded. It was unbelievable. Like nothing I've ever seen. It went on for miles, nothingness, like a mirror. I could see the curve of the earth. You loose all perspective and it looks like people are taking their next step off the edge of the world. You can also take funny photos. The weather was hot, the water warm, the salt crystals were sharp on my feet. We ate llama chops for lunch while sitting on top of our jeep. It was truly beautiful, like nothing I've ever seen before. It was the highlight of the trip.

We started to drive back and things got a little sketchy. Our tour company didn't have any pickups at the border scheduled for the next day, so they sold us to a different tour company. They split up our group of 6 in two two groups of three, mostly so they could fit extra paying passengers into the jeeps. They put us in separate hostels, without telling us they would and then were very light on details about what was happening with our friends. It was sketchy, but everything was completely fine and would have been fixed with a 5 minute walk & helpful two sentences from our guides.

The next morning we drove back to the Chilean border and back into San Pedro. It was an amazing trip that included things I've never seen before. It gave me time to recharge and think about what really matters in life. No Internet, TV and other modern conveniences. It was great.

UYUNI 2014

I started my trip from San Pedro de Atacama in Chile, booking the three day tour to the Salar de Uyuni. I'd done this trip before in 2011, but I still loved doing it again. You can read horror stories about this trip, but both times I've gone, I've never had a problem. This time I booked with Cordillera Traveller on the Chilean side and the accommodations were much better than with Colque Tours in 2011. We paid about $20 more than the competition but our driver seemed safer and more knowledgable.

I joined a group of 18 people in four Jeeps and we left San Pedro at 8am and made the one hour trek to the Bolivian border, where pretty much the only people who cross are tourists. We climbed from 2000 meters all the way up to 5000m (~16,000 feet) by nightfall. The scenery, along with the altitude, is (literally) breathtaking. We slept at altitude, but kept waking up every hour or so, our hearts racing and throats dry from the altitude.

The next day, we went past geysers, interesting rock formations and more colored lagoons until we reached a tiny town called Culpina K. It looked like a ghost town. Our guide, Humberto, told us that most of the people in the town either cultivate quinoa or work in the mines, so they got to bed by sundown at the latest. It was like going back in time to when most people farmed and lived in small towns.

We woke up early and drove through Uyuni, a poor, broken down town in the middle of nowhere, that wouldn't exist without the Salar that's just next door. At 10,000 square km, its the largest salt flat in the world and contains 50%-70% of the world's lithium supply.It's so different from anything I've ever seen and coming back a second time just brought the point home again. It's so flat, so white and so big that you can see the curve of the earth. On cloudy days, the guides can't go too far away from the "shore" or they risk getting disoriented and lost on the Salar. Not taking my own advice from 2011, I got burned to a crisp. Again.

We arrived back to Uyuni in the afternoon, burned, thirsty and caked in salt and went directly to the bus depot to reserve tickets to Potosí. Bolivian roads are unsafe. Drivers aren't very experienced, road conditions vary and you have to keep your eye out for mudslides and the occasional llama darting into the road. As a rule in Bolivia, always buy the most expensive bus ticket. Our bus trundled out of Uyuni onto the brand new road that connects Uyuni-Potosí-Sucre and prepared ourselves for the four hour trip. It was the first paved road we'd seen in four days and had only been completed in the past year. The bus seemed safe enough, but it was easy to imagine the bus falling off the hairpin turns.

Here's a few tips for those who would like to go in the future:

1. Get a good guide. If coming from Chile, you buy your tickets in San Pedro. Spend the extra money for a better tour guide and better accommodations if you have extra budget. The extra $20 is totally worth it.
2. Bring a sleeping bag. The hostels can be frigid at night. I'm glad I brought mine.
3. Bring lots of layers. It goes from cold in the morning to hot in the afternoon. My $12 wool sweater was a great purchase.
4. Bring at least 5L of bottled water per person. We brought 7L/person and finished it all in five days.

5. Bring toilet paper. The bathrooms are pretty bad in most of the hostels and usually don't have any. I went outside and so did most of the girls.
6. Bring snacks like chocolate, nuts and cookies for quick energy on the road. The altitude and wind takes it out of you.
7. Chew coca leaves and try coca tea to relieve your headaches. Don't drink alcohol until the 2nd or third day.
8. Try to get a group. There were many cars that were international mixes who couldn't communicate with the guide or each other. There was a car of 4 Koreans and 2 Hungarians, none of whom spoke Spanish or English. It wouldn't be nearly as fun as our car that had 7 people who could communicate in English/Spanish. If you're solo, try to join a group where you'll be able to share a language.
9. Offer your driver snacks, he'll love you for it. Tip him at the end.

Get Bolivianos in Chile, the exchange rate is much better and you'll have them to use at the border if necessary.

SECTION 10

Potosí & Sucre, Bolivia

Bolivia, wedged between Chile, Peru, Paraguay, Argentina and Brazil, is an amazing country of contrasts. With unmatched deposits of silver, tin, zinc, natural gas and enough lithium to power all of our modern devices for centuries, Bolivia should be a wealthy country. But is one of the poorest countries in the western hemisphere, only slightly better off than Haiti.

Since its "discovery" by the Spanish in the 1500s until today, Bolivia has been screwed over by nearly everyone, first by Spain, then Britain, the United States, Chile, Brazil, Paraguay and Argentina, all in partnership with its small upper class that has exploited its natural resources a labor. As I traveled through Bolivia over the past ten days, taking in its incredibly natural beauty, I read A Concise History of Bolivia and reread Open Veins of Latin America and began to appreciate just how unlucky the Bolivians have been.

Potosí

We arrived safely into Potosí and got off at the "ex terminal", which is really just a service station in the middle of the town and took a taxi to the Tukos

Casa Real, an old building that's been refurbished into a hotel. The room was massive, had hot water and the hotel provided a nice breakfast and only cost $40 per night for something that would cost at least $150 in the US. My heart was pounding and I was struggling to breath after walking up the three flights of stairs to get to the room. The 4060m altitude really takes it out of you. I can't imagine playing a world cup qualifier in La Paz, Quito or even Mexico City.

Potosí was the city that drove Europe's economy for almost three hundred years. From 1550-1783, it's estimated that 45,000 tons of pure silver came out of Cerro Rico, one of the richest silver mines in the history of the world. The mine made people fabulously wealthy and the town grew to a peak of 200,000 people at a time when Madrid only had about 50,000. But it was all built on exploitation of natives and africans, who were used as slaves. Some people estimate that eight million people have died in Cerro Rico mining first silver, then tin and now zinc.

The mine created incredible wealth, which led to some amazing churches, cathedrals, public spaces and houses, much of which has gone into different stages disrepair after the richest minerals were extracted. Cerro Rico's riches pushed the Spanish to create Bolivia's first national mint, which has been preserved and converted into a beautiful museum. The original donkey powered minting machines are preserved alongside some of the original coins.

The cathedral has been beautifully restored over the past ten year. During the war for independence, Simon Bolivar ordered the colorful cathedral to be whitewashed. People forgot and the incredible colors were rediscovered during the renovation. Now a UNESCO world heritage site, parts of colonial Potosí have been preserved, but the poverty remains.

Today, it's a loud, bustling city filled with diesel busses that come directly from China after they've been banned for expelling too much pollution, broken down cars honking at every intersection and people everywhere. I only saw a few non-natives during my three days in Potosí. Even today, an estimated 25% of Bolivians aren't fluent in Spanish and many people are still bilingual Quechua or Ayamar speakers, including a taxi I got into.

You can see the grinding poverty: Potosí is now one of Bolivia's poorest areas. There's hardly any industry, other than mining, and the occasional tourist, so locals, mostly indigenous people, are forced into the mines. The miners forced out the government's nationalization attempt because of rampant corruption, so now the miners have an elaborate series of cooperatives where you work for yourself. If you strike it rich, you can be a millionaire. If not, you may starve to death or be relegated to extreme poverty.

Because life expectancy is so short and families are large, Bolivia is an incredibly young country, with an average age of 22, compared to 33 in Chile and 36 in the US. It's noticeable. There are school aged kids everywhere, decked out in formal school uniforms. After school, the kids held massive water balloon and squirt gun fights on the main roads and plazas. I got caught in the crossfire a few times.

The food reflects the local conditions, making the most out of less expensive ingredients to provide the highest level of nutrition possible. There's lots of potatoes, quinoa, corn and vegetables. Meat is a luxury. Llama features on many menus. Coca Cola is ubiquitous, but I didn't see many international chain fast food restaurants.

We tried to go to Doña Eugenia, a restaurant specializing in local food, but it was closed. We ended up at a tiny restaurant nearby where I tried Kalapulca, a corn based soup with bits of meat and potatoes that's served with two super hot rocks that creates a volcano like soup. Another good option was Koala Cafe, which has cheap fixed price menus and featured an awesome quinoa soup.

We did a mine tour with Big Deal Tours, the best company in town. Founded and run by ex-miners, the guides take you on a 3km walk underground through the mine. I felt a bit conflicted about doing a mine tour to basically gawk at people who were working in terrible conditions, but after talking to the miners at the tour agency, I decided to do it. I'm glad I did. It was a sobering tour.

Miners still work nearly the same as they did in the 1500s. Most don't have electricity, so they use pickaxes, hammers and dynamite to bust open the rocks. They carry out the ore on their backs in 40-50kg loads or in wheeled carts weighing between one and two tons. If they slip, they get crushed. Life expectancy for miners is between 40 and 50.

It's dark, dank and filled with ankle deep water. Particles hang in the air, invading your lungs. Miners chew massive amounts of coca leaves to suppress hunger, fatigue and keep them energized, just like the slaves and exploited indigenous did in the colonial era. They drink 96% pure alcohol that costs the same as a beer to dull the pain and for luck to get "pure" veins of minerals and make sacrifices to "El Tio" the God who has domain of the mountain.

We started at the miners' market where we purchased gifts for the miners: coca leaves, juice and dynamite. A full dynamite kit (detonator, accelerant and stick) cost $3. As we walked through the mine, crouching down to try to avoid smashing our heads, and not doing so very well, we ran into miner after miner. They all looked similar. Dirty, old clothes. A huge wad of coca leaves. Many missing teeth. Upbeat. Happy to chat with us.

"How old are you?" asked our group to a miner who looked at least 35.

"Twenty-five," he replied.

"How much do you make per week?" we asked.

"About 1000 Bolivianos per week," he replied, which is about $140 per week.

"And how long have you been working in the mine?" we all wanted to know.

"Fifteen years," he said.

His story is fairly typical. There are so few jobs and money is so tight that fathers bring their sons to the mine starting at as young as ten. Or if the father dies and there's many kids, the oldest kids have to go into the mine to support the family.

After a three hour tour or just walking through the mine I was exhausted. The 4400m altitude didn't help, but the crouching, the head smashing and shuffling through water sapped my energy. I can't imaging having to hammer all day, run away from dynamite explosions and having to push 1-2 tons carts manually out of the mine for long shifts, with hunger pangs that are only dulled by coca leaves and alcohol.

I'm really glad I got to see Potosí, but it was incredibly sad to see a place that had such natural wealth that has been exploited and squandered to the point where its inhabitants live such a hard life.

Sucre

We decided to leave Potosí via the new bus terminal, which is located about twenty minutes from the town center. It's brand new and clearly is an investment from the central government, as the location clearly wasn't chosen for business reasons. We got out of the taxi and immediately felt like we were in a zombie movie. There were ticket sellers bleating like sheep, but there weren't any customers. The zombies activated and attacked from all sides, trying to get the commission on the $4 bus tickets. Check out the video.

After getting past the zombies, we settled into the four hour bus ride down from 4060m to Sucre's 2800m above sea level. Getting off the bus was like being able to drink the air. We took a taxi from the bus station to Hostal de Su Merced, a four star hotel in a refurbished building right downtown. It cost about $60 per night for a level of service that would cost $175+ in the US or Chile.

The first thing I noticed was the architecture. Everything is white. Sucre was Bolivia's capital during colonial times until the seat of government was changed to La Paz during one of Bolivia's many coups, dictatorships and revolutions and has preserved its historical buildings. The center is designated a UNESCO world heritage site, so there are building restrictions to keep the local character. The main square is surrounded by the cathedral, the municipality and the house where Bolivia's declaration of independence was signed. There are a multitude of churches and church buildings, schools and universities, including South America's first law school.

Although Sucre is a tourist city, the attractions are only open from about 10am-12pm, then again from 2pm-5pm, at most. It was frustrating, but by the second day I'd figured it out. Just like in other parts of Bolivia, the daily schedule is very different from Chile or what you might think of a Latin schedule. Shops open early and lunch ends by 1pm. Dinner is from 7-9 and most restaurants are closed by 9 or 930. People are out drinking at bars by 930pm. In Chile, people are just starting to eat dinner! It's another example in the long list that show Latin America is not just one homogeneous cultural unit.

I really enjoyed salteñas, Bolivian empanadas, especially from El Patio Salteñaria. They have a sweet, flaky dough and have a bit of sugar on the top and are filled with meat and vegetables. The filling is similar to a Chilean empanada de pino, but the dough is completely different. People eat salteñas from breakfast until lunch and not in the afternoon, whereas in Chile empanadas are a lunch or later food. It was hard to find high quality food, but I really enjoyed Condor Cafe, Cafe Mirador, and especially Cafe El Tapado, where I tired a variety of local, quinoa heavy dishes.

I had an amazing time in Bolivia. The country is absolutely beautiful, the people are welcoming and warm and the country just oozes with history. I hope Bolivia has better luck and better leadership as it moves into this century, as it has all of the natural resources to be much better developed than it is today.

SECTION 11

Colombia: Bogotá, Medellin & Cartagena

I wrote a blog post in 2012 about a trip to Colombia, then wrote a new one in 2016 after seeing Colombia's transformation. Check out the first post and compare and contrast my experiences.

Last month, I headed off to Colombia's Caribbean coast with six Chilean friends for some much needed vacation. Through a fluke of holidays, my friends could take a two week trip with only 5 days off from their jobs. Colombia is in the middle of some amazing changes: double digit economic growth, improved safety everywhere except near the Panama and Venezuela borders. Construction's everywhere. Lots of tourism. No noticeable violence. Less corruption. If you have a chance, it's worth checking out.

Many people in the US think that South American countries have similar cultures, but it can't be farther from the truth. Colombians are very different from Chileans. They're open, easygoing, cheerful, love to talk. They seem less classist. They're happy to smile at you on the street and generally give good customer service. They seem to be more entrepreneurial: I never once saw anyone begging for money, they were always trying to sell something, whether it was a piece of gum, tours, trinkets or even prostitutes.

Our flight to Cartagena stopped in Bogotá at 10pm and had a layover until 630am and we had no intention of staying cooped up in the airport all night. Nearly every Colombian directed us to Andres Carne de Res for dinner and drinks. Like all taxis in Colombia, our minibus taxi didn't have a meter and we negotiated our rate ahead of time. After 30 minutes, we arrived at the restaurant.

Andres Carne de Res is a loud, festive mix between a restaurant and a dance club. While the food wasn't that great and the prices were high, we had a great time just soaking in the atmosphere. After being in Chile for almost a year, it was a welcome experience. People were open, they smiled at you. The servers told jokes. People were happy and they showed it. They were drinking aguardiente and rum. They were dancing on the tables, in the aisles, everywhere. This was one of the only restaurants where we actually got exactly what we ordered. On the Caribbean coast, we'd be lucky to receive 50% of what we ordered. Many times there were substitutions (meat for chicken, fish for beef etc) without any comments.

After we left, we walked around a bit. It was a bit eerie. Not many people were out at 2am on a Thursday, as peoples get up and go to bed earlier than in Chile. I don't know if this is common or not, but we had to walk through metal detectors and get patted down to get into nearly all of the bars and restaurants in this area of the city. We had a good time, but were exhausted as we got back to the airport to fly to Cartagena. I'm going to have to go back to actually visit Bogota in the future.

CARTAGENA

I slept the entire flight from Bogota to Cartagena and still was wearing my heavy shirt and winter coat from Chilean winter as I got off the plane in Cartagena. BAM! I was slammed by a wall of heat and humidity that I couldn't escape until I got back to Chile. It was 80 degrees with 90% humidity at 8am! The first thing I noticed was music. It's everywhere. On the streets, in taxis, in restaurants. It floats from houses, pulses from plazas. You don't need headphones because Colombia has a soundtrack. And it's not just any type of music. It's happy, up beat, danceable. There's almost always at least one person dancing and it wasn't uncommon to walk past a pharmacy or convenience store and see the employees having an impromptu dance party.

We got to our hostel, Media Luna, and decided to explore. Cartagena is an old port city that oozes history. Starting in the 1500s, the Spanish used it as the main port to export gold, silver and other commodities from their South American colonies and built fortresses and city walls to defend it. Throughout the years it was held by the Spanish, by British pirates, attacked by the french, used as a slave trading outpost and much more. Walking through the brightly painted buildings behind the city walls, you can imagine pirates coming ashore to party or the Spanish counting their gold.

There's not much to do in Cartagena other than walk around. The center is dominated by upscale boutique hotels, high end restaurants and expensive international chain stores and the other parts are dominated by backpackers hostels. Our hostel was a beautifully converted mansion with a small swimming pool. It was full of backpackers, didn't have locks on the rooms, but served our purposes. If you want to party, stay here. If not, stay somewhere else.

I wasn't that big of a fan of the city, as the beaches weren't that nice, but the worst part were the sex and drug tourists and the prevalence of those willing to fulfill those vices. We ran into a middle aged Italian who destroyed a shop and wreaked havoc at our hostel as he was high out of his mind on cocaine. Two Australians who were sharing a prostitute for the week. Middle aged British guys negotiating prostitute prices on the street. Pickpockets, prostitutes and drug dealers seemed to be everywhere. And it was hot and humid. We had a great time with our fellow tourists, but it just wasn't my style. After a few days, it was time to move on to Tayrona.

TAYRONA NATIONAL PARK

We got up at 5am to catch a bus to Tayrona National Park. I slept the entire four hour drive and when I got off the bus, we were at the entrance to the park in the middle of nowhere. There were a few shops and we had breakfast, including a lulo juice which ended up being my favorite. We entered the park and started to walk. It was about and hour and half on a path through humid rainforest, then onto pristine white sand beaches on the Caribbean. By the time I got to camp, I looked like I'd been in a downpour. We had the option of staying in tents, hammocks or in a cabin with fans, full bathrooms and electricity. Since there were 7 of us and low season, it wasn't that much more expensive than getting 7 tents. It was the right choice. The tents were miserable because the humid air didn't move at night and we were subjected to intense tropical downpours for about 2 hours per day. Plus the bugs. Anyone who slept outside got eaten alive.

Colombians are much more formal than Chileans and that point was hammered home when we saw three Colombian friends from Medellin interacting with each other. One guy was annoyed at the other and said "no me gusta la manera en que usted me esta tratando," the English equivalent would be "sir, I don't like the way you are treating me." All my Chilean friends looked at each other, expecting his friend to give him shit for being so formal, but just said "lo siento, tiene razón" "I'm sorry, you're right." In Chile or the US, friends would never dream of saying that to each other. They'd say say some variation of "dude stop being a dick." We saw other examples of Colombia formality that was really different from what I've gotten used to in Chile.

Tayrona was tied for my favorite part of the trip. The national park consists of multiple pristine white sand beaches with warm tropical water. There are a few small shacks that serve food, but otherwise it's not developed. They had all of the fresh fruit you could imagine in tropical sizes that were 4x what I'm used to seeing. I learned to love 75 cent Aguila beers, arepas, plantains and tropical fruit juice. There were lots of tourists from all over the world, but the park is big enough that you have privacy, time to think, hang out, swim. At one of the beaches fish would just swim up and nibble at your feet. The whole park was incredibly relaxing. I did absolutely nothing but swim and eat amazing fish and fruit for three days. Although I could have stayed longer, we decided to move onto Taganga the next day.

We took a 45 minute speedboat ride over to Taganga from Tayrona and arrived in a small beachside town of about ~1000. It had a really strange vibe: lots of tourists and lots of locals selling pretty much anything to tourists. We stayed at Hostel Benjamin, the only place with hot water, AC and a pool. Its a nice place run by Israelis who went on their trip after their military service and decided to stay. The place is clearly catered to other Israelis, of which there are tons in Taganga, but we were welcomed with open arms.

TAGANGA

It's got an even stranger vibe than the town itself, with drugged out Israelis listening to psytrance at all hours of the day. The entire town has an eerie feel straight out of a movie that I can't quite describe. Between little kids trying to sell us drugs and women, to local girls speaking Hebrew/English/French to "cater" to the travelers and foreigners of all nationalities there to party, it just wasn't my scene. I also witnessed the phenomenon of local girls who didn't consider themselves prostitutes but would charge guys "if they thought the guys was disposed to pay." Really strange. It just didn't sit right with me, but we had a great time because we took day trips to incredible beaches each day instead of staying in the city.

ISLA BARU

We took the death bus back to Cartagena from Taganga. I call it the death bus because Colombians are crazy drivers. They don't obey road signs, lane markers or right of way. I consider myself a good driver, but I would have had problems on this "highway." The road went to a single lane from time to time and drivers steamed ahead, blaring their horn to warn anyone in their way. People passed without warning. Our driver dozed off multiple times with sheer drop offs to the right only to pull back at the last moment. I put my life in the hands of the driver and just went to sleep.

We made it to Cartagena and then onto Isla Baru. The place was packed. Completely full of people. We were led to believe it was a small beach with no electricity, hammocks, a place to get away. As we arrived, I couldn't imagine staying 3 days with all those people. Luckily, they were all day trippers. As they left, maybe only 100 people stayed overnight. This was my favorite part of the trip. No electricity besides some generators, fresh fish, white sand beaches, warm water, shooting stars. It was perfect. We rented a cabin with real beds, but quickly realized that was a mistake. If you were out of the breeze, it was unbearable. I slept in a hammock and then under the stars covered in mosquito nets and was perfect. My friends who stayed in the beds slept horribly and were eaten alive. The only drawback were the locals who tried to sell you everything. Aggressively. It got tiresome, but if you ignored them, they went away.

We saw sex tourism on display yet again. A middle aged Mexican who the locals claimed was a narco trafficker had rented the best room above a restaurant for himself and his entourage, which consisted of three body guards and four Colombian prostitutes. He'd drink 2 liters of Absolut per day and had trouble walking anytime after about 10am. He'd force his help to bring his mattress right to the waters edge so he could "hang out" with his prostitutes under the cover of darkness. He bitched out one of his bodyguards worse than I've ever heard anyone bitch anyone out in my life. This guy and the bugs were the only downside of Isla Baru.

The coolest part of Isla Baru happened at night. After a day of relaxing on the beach, we bought a few bottles of rum and drank under the stars. One of the locals came over and told us we had to check out the water at night. He wouldn't tell us why. We dubiously walked over to the water and splashed around. The water lit up. There's an algae in the water that when irritated, light up like little LEDs. It was incredibly beautiful. No lights, glowing water and shooting stars. Perfect. I tried again sober the next night and it was just as cool.

Our last day, we took a tiny boat around the islands and ended up on a tiny island where we docked in a bay. We had fresh caught crabs and lobsters right from the bay, drinking fresh drinks out of coconuts. If I ever go back, I'd spend more time on these small islands than on the more developed beaches and cities.

Overall, I had an amazing time. I didn't bring a working phone, had internet for about three days total and just let my mind go blank. It was great to get closer to a group of friends who I've know for awhile. I met some incredible people and really liked the Colombians I met. I'd love to go back to to check out Bogota and Medellin. I have a feeling the country is going to be one the stars of South America over the next few decades.

COLOMBIA'S INCREDIBLE TRANSFORMATION AND THE MEDELLIN MIRACLE

I'm just back from my third trip to Colombia since 2012. Before my first trip, I didn't know what to expect and wrote the travelogue you just finished reading. I came back in 2015 and 2016 and saw huge positive changes in Cartagena. I also went to Medellin, a beautiful city nestled in a mountain valley for the first time. This post compares my experience from 2012 with 2016 and talks about why Medellin is a hidden gem that's just starting to get its due both for tourism, but also as a potential tech hub in South America.

In 2012, a group of Chilean friends and I planned to go to Colombia's north coast for two weeks and hang out on its beautiful tropical beaches. I had studied a bit of Colombia in high school Spanish class, as my teacher was Colombian and wanted to share Colombia's natural beauty with us. Being high schoolers, most of us only wanted to learn about Pablo Escobar, the drug gangs, movies, the violence, the civil war, how someone could murder a soccer star after scoring an own goal (watch the documentary, its really good)...pretty much the only news about Colombia we ever heard in the US.

In college, I wrote a paper about the drug war, the hunt for Pablo Escobar and the violence that plagued Colombia in the 80s and 90s. Medellin was the most dangerous city in the world, with a murder rate of over 381 per 100,000, 20x more than 2015 Chicago and 7x more than the most dangerous cities in the US. It's now down almost 90% from its peak and is referred to as The Medellin Miracle.

My friends and I went to the north coast, landing in Cartagena, going to Santa Marta, Tayrona and Isla Baru. Some of my family and friends expressed concern about the trip, but I told them not to worry, Colombia was much safer and was growing quickly.

We didn't have any problems, but saw police corruption, lots of foreigner tourists in town for sex or drug tourism and underdeveloped, dangerous roads outside of the city. A few of our group got pick-pocked, and you almost always noticed that bit of an edge: if you said something to the wrong person, or were in the wrong place and the wrong time, you might end up in real trouble.

Fast forward three years later. I spent a few days in Cartagena and the difference is like night and day. There's hundreds of new apartment towers along the waterfront where there used to be crappy construction or nothing at all. The walled city is even more developed, with more restaurants and better lighting. It feels much safer. But the part that surprised me most was the part outside of the walled city, where I'd stayed before.

When I was there in 2012, most of the roads weren't paved, the only accommodations were cheap party hostels. The streets were lined with drug dealers, military police and prostitutes, many of them working together.

In 2015, that's all gone, at least from public view. The roads are paved, the infrastructure seems better. And there's countless boutique hotels and interesting restaurants that have opened up to serve ever increasing numbers of tourists. Even the taxis seemed to have gotten an upgrade!

On that same trip in 2015, I spent time in Medellin and Bogota, this time for a mix of business and vacation. I hadn't been to Medellin before, but had been watching Narcos to see a bit more about how things might have worked in the 80s and 90s. I didn't really know what to expect and some of my family and friends still had the same idea about Colombia: that it's dangerous, full of narcos, guerrillas and corrupt police.

Upon arrival, I quickly realized Medellin didn't deserve that reputation anymore. The Medellin Miracle has reduced the murder rate by ~90%, opened up development opportunities and made the city a better place.

Medellin, know as the city of eternal spring, is a South American gem that's just starting to get discovered by tourists. Nestled into a lush, green, mountain valley, Medellin has the same weather is the same all year round: 70s-80s and a bit of humidity. The locals say it's a place you can pick your weather: want it a bit colder? Go up into the mountains a bit. Like it really hot? Go down into the valley some more. It rains tropically for part of the day during the rainy season, but otherwise is the perfect climate.

Cost of living is incredibly low. It would be hard to spend $2000 a month living in Medellin full time, living in the best areas of town in an apartment with beautiful views, living an incredible lifestyle. And you could certainly have a great lifestyle for $1000.

Backpackers have been coming to Medellin for years, but over the past few years, tourism is booming, along with a bourgeoning startup scene supported by talented engineering talent, talented entrepreneurs, smart venture capitalists, all helped on by Ruta N, a public/private program that gives grants to help entrepreneurs and tech people be successful.

I was just in Medellin again two weeks ago and the city keeps getting better. New infrastructure, restaurants and bars are opening up, nightlife is continuing to improve, startups, both from Colombia and abroad are expanding and more tourists are coming. Located 5 hours NYC, 7 from LA and Chicago, 3 from Miami, and 5 from Santiago and Buenos Aires, 3 from Lima, it's uniquely positioned to take off as a place for tourism and to do business.

While Medellin is still clearly more dangerous than Chile or nice parts of major US cities, I never felt in danger riding public transport, taking taxis, and going to a night time soccer game. There's still petty crime, drugs are readily available if you want them and there's a bit of an edge in some places, but if you don't get completely trashed and keep your wits, you'll most likely be fine, just like in any other big city. There are still very dangerous parts of the country, mostly in areas where the ELN and FARC still have very strong influence near the Venezuelan and Ecuadorian borders, but most tourists don't go there. The government has been negotiating with the guerrillas to end the world's longest civil war. Most Colombians I talked to were sick of the conflict and ready for peace. They were hopeful that the peace treaty would be signed and that it would hold.

I'm really bullish on Medellin both as a bourgeoning tourist destination and also as one of Latin America's startup hubs, and Colombia as a country. It's a large market, close to the US, with interesting, open, fun people and some of the most incredible natural landscapes in the world. I'll be spending more time there in the future.

Montevideo, Punta del Este, Punta del Diablo, Velizas

Uruguay is a small country of about 4m people sandwiched between Argentina and Brazil. Nearly half live in Montevideo, the capital. It sort of feels like an upscale, more laid back Argentina that actually works. People speak the same accented Spanish as they do in Argentina, but with seemingly less slang. I took an eight day trip last month during Carnaval for a short vacation.

I arrived into the Montevideo airport, tried to rent a car, but couldn't find anything, so I immediately took a bus directly to Punta del Este, hoping to find a car there. I hadn't realized when I booked the flight that it was going to be Carnaval in Uruguay, but that explained why everything was busy.

Punta del Este is the French Rivera of South America. South Americans with money come from all over to play on the beaches, eat in top restaurants and hobnob with each other. As such, it's really expensive, but there's great food and good beaches. Nearly everyone there was in good shape, extremely tan and fairly well dressed. It wasn't really my style, as Punta is very built up and feels a bit like Florida. After a day and a half it was time to move on.

I took a bus north along the coast to Punta del Diablo, a small town that gets overrun with tourists in the summer. One family used to own all of the land, but has now sold lots to developers for cabins, restaurants and small apartments. Since it was Carnaval and everyone had Monday and Tuesday off from work, the place was packed. It's really close to the Brazilian border and you can tell: Portuguese is everywhere, the merchants accept reales, caipirinhas are on every menu. They also accept Argentine pesos, but at 10 pesos to the dollar, or 2x the official rate. Argentinians were happy to pay.

Punta del Diablo has two huge beaches that were full close to town, but if you walked 10 minutes, you could find beaches with hardly anyone. It was hot and sunny, maybe 90 degrees, in the morning, but every late afternoon it got cold. Try to stay at a cabin instead of a hostel, they're about the same price.

The surf was pretty high, making the water seem colder than it was. There are tons of little restaurants, mostly catering to tourists. The best ones were farther into town, maybe 3 minutes walk. The first ones were touristy, kind of expensive and lower quality. My favorites were a Mexican cantina through the center of town and Il Tano Cucino, an Italian restaurant where the owner makes his own pasta and gnocchi outside each day. It was so good I went twice in one day.

At night during Carnaval, the city came alive. Local kids filled up anything they could find to have massive water fights with each other. Others took to ambushing tourists. My favorite was a kid with a hose who hid behind some bushes to spray people. After I got hit, I watched for 20 minutes as other got destroyed by the water.

Later on in the night, there were two parades with local kids dancing, singing and riding around in floats. Everyone followed the parades, dancing, singing and drinking until they arrived at the beach, between three bars. It morphed into a huge outside dance party with the occasional spray of water from some kids. Everyone was happy. You could tell the Brazilians apart from everyone else by how quickly they moved their feet.

After a few days in Punta del Diablo I went on a day trip to Velizas, about an hour to the south. It's a tiny town, much less developed than Punta del Diablo, but the beach was beautiful. The water was warm and there wasn't a cloud in the sky. Looking to the south, you can see the huge sand dunes of Cabo Polonio national park. I wished I'd spent a little more time there.

I spent my last two days in Montevideo. I found a great hotel on book-ing.com that happened to have a 65% discount in the old section of town with a view of the "sea." Although everyone calls it the sea, it's really the rio de la plata, which at Montevideo happens to be one of the widest rivers in the world. The old section is in the middle of being restored. There are boutique hotels, small shops, good restaurants and stores that are going into beautiful old buildings. Montevideo has some incredible architecture that is way better preserved than Santiago and the old city is going to be incredible in a few years as people start to move back.

I went for lunch at Mercado Central and sampled Medio y Medio, a half and half mix of white wine and champagne that really sneaks up on you. Uruguayans eat the fourth most beef per capita in the world and for good reason. Their steaks were incredible. Bar Fun Fun is a touristy but eclectic bar that's been in business since 1895, complete with live tango and music. At night, hardly anyone is around in the old city, except at a few bars. It was a little creepy and felt like a zombie movie, especially compared to the day when it's filled with people

I really liked Uruguay. The country seems stable, people are nice, the cities seemed safe and things seemed to work. People seem to have a really high quality of life. Montevideo is in the middle of gentrification and the old city will be incredible in about 5 years if they continue to make progress. I will definitely be back in the future.

SLANG

Chapter 16

Chilean Slang

Chileans use ridiculous amounts of slang that isn't used anywhere else in the world. Chileans will jokingly say "we don't speak Spanish here, we speak Chilean." There are literally hundreds of "Chilean" words and you'll learn them by asking Chileans and listening to conversations. Ask friends, taxi drivers, co-workers, really anyone who will listen, to explain what something means. Generally people are happy to see a foreigner learning their language. One of the strangest things for me is that Chileans continue to use slang as adults. In the US, we speak a ton of slang until we're maybe 25, then stop, except with our closest friends. In Chile, professional people use slang in the office and old men still use slang. It's part of the culture. Here's a quick overview of many common Chilean slang words:

The four most common words:

Weon

Ubiquitously used by all Chileans. Means anything from dude to guy to fucking asshole, depending on context. Can also be used as an adjective.

Weon weon weon weon is a full sentence that Chileans understand. Shouldn't be used in business context or polite context.

Wea

The closest translation is "thing," but it can be used to represent an object, a place, an idea, a situation, or even a person (very disrespectfully). Shouldn't be used in business or polite company.

Po

It doesn't really mean anything, it just adds emphasis. Si po is yes!

Cachai

It means "get it?" or "understand?" You'll hear it at the end of a sentence or at the beginning.

Additional Slang:
Carrete – Party
Taco – Traffic jam
Cuico – Upperclass (can be pejorative)
Flaite – Lowerclass (pejorative)
Piscola – Pisco and coke
Jugar la pelota – To play soccer
18 – Fiestas Patrias, on September 18th. National holidays
Asado – BBQ
Seco – A genius. Someone who's really good at something. Literally, dry.
Pasarse – To go overboard, to go beyond expectations
La micro – Metro busses
Guagua – Baby
Filete – Slang for awesome. Literally means steak
Pieza – Bedroom
Stickfix – Gluestick
Confor(t) – Toilet paper. A brand name, just like Kleenex in the US.
Bacán – Cool, awesome
Mula – Fake or liar
Pololeando – In a relationship.
Pololo/a – Boyfriend/girlfriend.
Caleta – A bunch, lots

Cuático – A big deal/unbelievable.

Luca – 1000 pesos.

Gamba – 100 pesos

Quina – 500 pesos

La roja – Chile's national soccer team

Chela – Beer

Michelada – Beer with lemon juice served in salt rimmed glass. Tabasco, Worcestershire sauce optional

Viejos – Parents

Gringo – Someone from the US or other English speaking countries

Piscolear – To drink piscolas

Un palo – One million pesos

Un palo verde – One million US dollars

Kuchen – Cake (especially in the south)

Un roto – Someone with no manners

Huaso – A country person

La dura – For real?

Brígido – Terrible

Jotear – To hit on, flirt

Jote – Someone who hits on girls. Named after a vulture like bird in the way it circles its prey

Chiquillo/(a) – Boy/girl

Agarrar – To hook up

Lata – Boring, pain in the ass. Literally can

Latero – A pain in the ass.

Dar jugo – Messing around, generally while drunk

Webear – To give someone a hard time, to make fun of them.

La cagada – A disaster

Colapsado – Over burdened

Chancha – Pig. Piggy

Chanta – Untrustworthy

Piola – Decent, calm, nice.

Chapter 17

Conclusion

Well that about covers it! You're now ready for your trip to Chile! Whether you're coming for a vacation, to study abroad, to start a business, because you married a Chilean or for any other reason, I really hope this book has been useful. The appendix contains specific information that may be useful to you, but not to everyone else. Check out my blog, www.nathanlustig.com, which has updated content, restaurant guides and up to date information for after you've purchased this book.

If you have questions about anything I covered or feedback on this book, I'd love to hear from you. Shoot me an email at nathanlustig@gmail.com or reach out to me on twitter @nathanlustig or via my blog http://www.nathanlustig.com and I'd be happy to chat.

If you're an entrepreneur looking to setup shop in Chile, please shoot me a message via www.MagmaPartners.com and I'll be happy to try to help you out.

Chapter 18

About the Author

I'm doing everything I can to stay out of the cubicle. I love sports(especially soccer), food and traveling, or any way to combine the three. I'm currently the Managing Partner of <u>Magma Partners</u>, the premier venture capital firm in Latin America.

In 2005, I bought ExchangeHut.com, after my freshman year at the University of Wisconsin, and transformed it from a local tickets and textbooks trading site with under 2,000 users to a profitable national business with over 125,000 users by the time I was a senior, leading to its acquisition by a publicly traded company in 2008.

A few months later, during my 2nd senior year, I teamed up with Jesse Davis to co-found Entrustet. Entrustet helps people access, transfer and delete online accounts after someone dies. We were featured in the NY Times, The Economist, TechCrunch, Mashable, Forbes, BBC and hundreds of others. In April 2012,Entrustet was acquired by SecureSafe, the market leader in digital estate planning and online data safes.

In November 2010, I moved to Santiago, Chile as the 7th team to participate in Startup Chile. It was an incredible experience and I wrote a ton of posts about my time in the program, including when I got give a speech in Spanish to Chile's president.

I love speaking with entrepreneurs and showing people that entrepreneurship is a potential choice for young people and that college can be the best time to start a company. I enjoy talking with people to try to give them the entrepreneurial push toward either starting a company or working for a startup. In May 2009, I founded Capital Entrepreneurs to bring the burgeoning startup community in Madison closer together. I'm also the cofounder of Madison's Forward Technology Conference and am a founding member of The Young Entrepreneur Council. To see what else I've been up to from 2000-2010, check out my decade in review on my blog.

I worked as head of marketing for Welcu, a Chilean startup that gives companies the tools they need to plan events and helped them grow from 7 to 40 people and open offices in Argentina, Colombia and Brazil.

You can follow me on Twitter (twitter.com/nathanlustig), find me on LinkedIn or send me a note through on my contact page on my blog.

SECTION 1

Acknowledgements

I'd like to thank the follow people who either helped me write this book or inspired certain sections. I couldn't have done it without you all. Thanks.

Jesse Davis
Laurie Eggert and Howard Lustig
Francisco Sáenz Rica
Felipe Rodriguez
Pedro Varas
Max Grekin
Pedro Navarro & Operación Colombia
Jesse Ball
Forrest & Sarah Woolworth
Camila Carreño
Alan Weschler
Bernardita Rios
Javiera Quiroga
Enrique Fernandez & Gonzalo Saieg
Jake Lustig

Nicolás Orellana, Sebastián Gamboa, Carito Orellana, Carla Gonzalez, Jaime Oyarzun, Alvaro Quezada & Team Welcu
Brenna Loury
Diego Philippi
Nicolás Shea, Jean Boudeguer, Cristián López & Team Startup Chile
George Cadena
Shahar Nechmads
Juan Pablo Salas
Tiago Matos
Vijay Kailas
Nancy Eggert
Leah Lustig
Raj Uttamchandani
Juan Pablo Tapia
Maxine Liang
Vijay Kailas
Daniel Undurraga
José Tomás Marabio
Skinner Layne
Scott Jones
Pablo Gutierrez
David Lloyd

SECTION 2

Photo Credits

Chapter 1 – Nathan Lustig

Chapter 2 – Nathan Lustig/Start-Up Chile

Chapter 3 – Sarah Stierch

    Chapter 3.1 – Tjeerd Wiersma

    Chapter 3.2 – German Poo-Caamaño – https://www.flickr.com/photos/gpoo/

    Chapter 3.3 – Dr. Wendy Longo – https://www.flickr.com/photos/wtlphotos/

    Chapter 3.4 – jonjomckay – https://www.flickr.com/photos/jonjomckay/

    Chapter 3.5 – Alexisnyal – https://www.flickr.com/photos/alexisnyalphotography/

    Chapter 3.6 – Ron Bennetts – https://www.flickr.com/photos/ronbennetts/

    Chapter 3.7 – Carlos Varela – https://www.flickr.com/photos/c32/

    Chapter 3.8 – European Southern Observatory

Chapter 4 – Dr. Wendy Longo – https://www.flickr.com/photos/wtlphotos/

Chapter 5 – Osmar Valdebenito – https://www.flickr.com/photos/b1mbo/

Chapter 6 – Moyan Brenn – https://www.flickr.com/photos/aigle_dore/

    Chapter 6.1 – William Hook – https://www.flickr.com/photos/williamhook/

    Chapter 6.2 – Chris Potter – https://www.flickr.com/photos/86530412@N02/

Chapter 6.3 – <u>Spiros Vathis</u>
Chapter 7 – Sarah Stierch – <u>https://www.flickr.com/photos/sarahvain/</u>
Chapter 8 – Alessandro Vasaturo – <u>https://www.flickr.com/photos/alessandro_vasaturo/</u>
Chapter 9 – <u>Klausiee</u>
    Chapter 9.1 – Ken Sutton – <u>https://www.flickr.com/photos/kene1/</u>
    Chapter 9.2 – Gobierno de Chile / Start-Up Chile
    Chapter 9.3 – Tendenci Software – <u>https://www.flickr.com/photos/tendenci/</u>
    Chapter 9.4 – Nathan Lustig
    Chapter 9.7 – Jumpseller.com
Chapter 10 – <u>Ryan Maple</u>
Chapter 11 – <u>HackNY.org</u>
Chapter 12 – Google Maps
    Chapter 13.1 – Carlos Varela – <u>https://www.flickr.com/photos/c32/</u>
    Chapter 13.2 – Thomas S. – <u>https://www.flickr.com/photos/95786359@N05/</u>
    Chapter 13.3 – <u>DSanchez17</u>
Chapter 14 – 401(k) 2012 – <u>https://www.flickr.com/photos/68751915@N05/</u>
Chapter 15 – Dr. Wendy Longo – <u>https://www.flickr.com/photos/wtlphotos/</u>
    Chapter 15.1 – Fallen Constellation – <u>https://www.flickr.com/photos/fallen_constellation/</u>
    Chapter 15.2 – Andrej – <u>https://www.flickr.com/photos/adundovi/</u>
    Chapter 15.3 – Melenama – <u>https://www.flickr.com/photos/21856521@N07/</u>
    Chapter 15.4 – Nathan Lustig
    Chapter 15.5 – Juan de Dios Santander Vela – <u>https://www.flickr.com/photos/juandesant/</u>
    Chapter 15.6 – Gaspar Abrilot – <u>https://www.flickr.com/photos/gasabrilot/</u>
    Chapter 15.7 – Rodrigo Paredes – <u>https://www.flickr.com/photos/rodrigoparedes/</u>
    Chapter 15.8 – Paige Brown
    Chapter 15.9 – Nathan Lustig
    Chapter 15.10 – Nathan Lustig
    Chapter 15.11 – Bryan Pocius – <u>https://www.flickr.com/photos/pocius/</u>
    Chapter 15.12 – Vince Alongi – <u>https://www.flickr.com/photos/vincealongi/</u>
Chapter 16 – <u>Buzzword Bingo</u>
Chapter 18 – Nathan Lustig

Chapter 19

Appendix

SECTION 1

How to renew your Chilean Temporary Visa

Your temporary visa lasts for one year from when you arrived and will expire if you do nothing. This means your RUT will expire and you won't be able to conduct business in Chile. Also, if you stay in Chile past your visa, you will have to pay a fine as you are leaving.

The process to renew your Chilean work visa is not that difficult, but it can be confusing and time consuming. Here's what I did to renew my visa in November 2011. I know a few other friends did the same process and had success. Please verify that this information is up to date before you rely on it, but I believe it to be current as of Oct 1, 2012.

You should start the renewal process 2-3 months before your visa is set to expire.

1. Review the information from the Chilean Extranjeria.

You must decide if you would like to extend your visa (prorrogar) or apply for permanent residency. It is much easier to apply for a visa extension, so if you've only been in Chile one year, I'd suggest applying for the extension

Note: Depending on your nationality, applying for permanent residency can have adverse tax implications, so consult with an attorney or accountant who will be able to advise you.

2. Review the Requirements to Extend (Prorrogar) your Chilean Work Visa

You will need the following information:

- Your completed application form that you printed off from the government website. Note: In box #9, check the "prorroga de visa-ción" box
- Three 2cm × 3cm photos with your name and RUT on the bottom. Any photo shop should be able to do this for you. Ask for foto carnet con nombre y RUT.
- A photocopy of the front and back of your carnet
- A photocopy of passport photo page
- A photocopy of previous visa that is in your passport
- 1 photocopy of *Certificado de Registro,* which you get from the *Policía Internacional* (Morandé No 672, Santiago Centro). You can potentially use a copy of the half page paper we got from the police when we first got here, but to be safe, go get a new one.
- *Certificado de antecedentes* from *Servicio de Registro Civil e Identificación de Chile* issued within the last 30 days. There are many offices in Santiago where you can get them, including the one on Huerfanos. Go to registro civil and click oficinas for a full list.

3. Include additional supporting documentation

Chile wants to renew your visa. At its most basic, Chile prefers skilled immigrants and wants to make sure that visa holders won't end up living in the streets, participating in anti-government protests, committing crimes or asking the government for money. In addition to all of that information, I included the following documentation. I suggest you think about including the same. All documents translated into Spanish:

1. My professional resume
2. A list of all of the things I've done in Chile
3. Any press I've gotten in Chile or abroad
4. A one page letter explaining why I wanted to stay in Chile

5. A copy of documents showing that you have either incorporated in Chile or plan to incorporate. If you have already incorporated, send documents showing that you're up to date on your taxes and all fees. Showing an office address is helpful as well.
6. An executive summary of my business
7. If you are employed by a company here in Chile, include your employment contract.
8. If you don't have a business incorporated here or an employment contract check the box "trabajando por cuenta propia." I've heard that it's harder to get renewed without a company or an employment contract, but it can be done.
9. A copy of my original Startup Chile invitation letter
10. An overview of my personal finances including copies of my Chilean bank statements and current balances in selected foreign accounts.

4. Send all of this by certified mail (Correo Certificado) to:

SEÑORES:
SOLICITUD TEMPORARIA CLASIFICADOR N° 8
CORREO CENTRAL SANTIAGO

Note: Some people have had success going to the office in your region where you are living and delivering the documents in person. If you are able to do this, it's better than waiting for the documents by mail, but many have been turned away. It's worth a shot to try it in person.

5. Wait for your visa en trámite confirmation

You will get a piece of paper that says your visa is "en trámite" and you'll need to take this paper with you if you want to leave the country. Chile's computer system is not connected together, so the only way to leave and enter without paying fines or paying for a new visa is to bring this paper along with you.

If you have more questions, check out the extranjeria website or feel free to email me.

How to Apply for Chilean Permanent Residence

The entire process takes 6-7 months from when you first apply to when it's granted or denied. They accept English applications, but in my opinion it makes sense to translate everything. If your Spanish is bad, pay someone to translate your application.

Step 1 – Review Previous Visa Requirements

You must have already had a temporary visa for at least one year and have spent at least six months of that temporary visa in Chile. If you don't meet this criteria, you must apply for another temporary visa. You're only able to apply for a temporary visa twice, after that you must apply for a permanent residence. If you don't meet the previous visa requirements, the extranjeria tells you that you should apply for the permanent residence anyway and then appeal if it's denied.

Step 2 – Review Application deadlines

You can first apply 90 days before your temporary visa expires. Do this as early as possible to minimize time you have with an expired carnet. More on this later.

Step 3 – Go to Extranjeria website to pick your visa type

If you have your own business, Inversionista is likely the best one for you, but there are many other options. If you get confused or don't know which one best fits your criteria, go to extranjeria in person and ask. They were very helpful every time I went and had questions.

Step 4 – Review the requirements.

Here are the requirements for Inversionista. You can find the rest of the requirements for permanent visas here.

Step 5 – Fill out forms

Download the current Residencia Definitiva document (pdf) from Extranjeria and fill it out.

Step 6 – Get Certificado de Antecedentes from Registro Civil

You can do this online if you've already registered in the system or you have to go to a Registro Civil in person.

Step 7 – Get Certificado de Viajes from Policia de Investigaciones (PDI)

This document shows how long you've been out of the country during your last visa. Go to PDI offices at Morandé 672. This tramite costs CLP$800 and you usually have to wait at least an hour, sometimes more. It's open from 830-1400.

Step 8 – Get all your paperwork

- Copy of both sides of your carnet
- Copy of certificado de registro. You can use your certificado from last year or pay another CLP$800 from the PDI to get a new one when you're getting your certificado de viajes.
- Copy of your passport with all ID pages and any pages with Chilean visas or stamps. I just copied the entire thing.
- Three 3×2 color photos with your name and RUT

Step 9 – Write your personal statement

You need to write a personal statement why you'd like to stay in Chile. I included my resume, everything I've done in Chile, any press clippings from Chilean newspapers and my plans to stay in Chile, plus bank information showing that I would not become dependent on the state if they granted me the visa. My packet was about 15 pages long and the clerk in Extranjeria told me it was more than enough. Most people write a page and that's it.

Step 10 – Get business documentation (if Inversionista)

If you're doing the Inversionista visa for your own company or if you are an independent contractor you need to prove you are making money and have assets in Chile. You'll need:

- Copy of operating agreement (Escritura) of your Chilean company
- Certificado de inicio de actividades from SII
- Your company's last 8 IVA payments
- Your company's last "balance tributario"
- Your company's last "declaracion de renta"
- Proof you've paid your company's patente
- Proof that you actually own stock in the company

If you're doing it as an independent contractor (emits boletas), you need to prove the same things as above, but with your own personal records.

Step 11 (optional) – Take everything to Extranjeria for a review

The clerks at Extranjeria are happy to go through your paperwork with you and tell you if everything is in order. I did this and realized I was missing a form, so for me it was worth it.

Step 12 – Mail all of this via Correo Certificado to:

SEÑORES: SOLICITUD PERMANENCIA DEFINITIVA CLASIFICADOR N° 8 CORREO CENTRAL SANTIAGO

Step 13 – Wait for "Visa en Tramite" temporary 6 month visa

Extranjeria says it will take 45 days and mine took exactly 45 days. If your old visa has expired (like mine did), you cannot reenter Chile on your old visa and must pay for a tourist visa if you enter before you get your "visa en tramite" paper work. You can check on your progress on the extranjeria autoconsulta website. Once you're approved as "en tramite" you can print off your form which allows you to travel on your temporary six month visa.

Note: you must bring that paper with you if you travel, as your carnet will be expired. Make sure you have it on your person, not in your luggage. I made this mistake once and had to convince someone from my flight to get my backpack from baggage claim for me while I was waiting with a PDI agent who was mocking me the entire time.

You will get a letter from Extranjeria that says that your visa is "en tramite" and that you're allowed to do any legal activity that you used to be able to do on your old visa, but no Chilean entity actually recognizes it, including:

- Entel
- VTR
- Movistar
- Claro
- SII
- Banks
- Anywhere that requires a valid carnet

Basically you can't do anything in Chile with your letter because nobody recognizes it. This was the most frustrating part of being between visas. I was carnetless from Nov 15th, 2012 until May 17th, 2013. If you have any official business, get it done before your carnet expires or else you're screwed.

Step 14 – Pay application fee

You have to pay a fee, depending on the visa you applied for, via bank check at any bank. Mine was ~$50.000 and I had to go in person to my bank to pay.

Step 15 – Wait for approval or denial

It took me another five months before I was approved. You can check again on the extranjeria autoconsulta website for news.

Step 16 – Go to Extranjeria with your visa acceptance form, carnet and passport and get your permanent visa

Step 17 – Go to PDI to register your address and get your certificado de residencia definitiva (CLP$800).

Step 18 – Go to registro civil to get your carnet (CLP$4.050)

Step 19 – Wait two weeks and go back to the registro civil to pick up your carnet

Step 20 – Drink a piscola to celebrate being a Chilean permanent resident and being done with all of these tramites!

Once you have the visa, you must either visit Chile once per year or you must go to a Chilean embassy once per year to renew your visa. If you go the embassy route, you'll need to come back to Chile once every four years to keep your visa valid, or else you lose it

Note: please review each step on your own, this is the process I used in 2012/2013 and may change without notice.

SECTION 3

Apartment Rental

Apartments

Two Start-Up Chile alumni and I started Andes Property to help foreigners find amazing furnished or unfurnished rentals or buy apartments. Contact us via contact@andesproperty.com or fill out our availability form on Andesproperty.com for more info.

SECTION 4

My Speech To President Piñera

Last Thursday, I had the opportunity to share my experiences of the last six months in Chile as part of the Startup Chile program at a breakfast with Geeks on a Plane, Startup Chile y the President of Chile, Sebastián Piñera.

When I arrived to Chile, I only spoke a little Spanish and I never thought in my wildest dreams that I'd have the opportunity to give a talk at a breakfast with the president, an audience of over 100 and the press. This is what I said the President Piñera and the rest of the audience.

Hi, my name is Nathan Lustig and I am the cofounder of Entrustet, the seventh company that arrived in Santiago for Startup Chile. I want to thank President Piñera for inviting us to this breakfast and for the opportunity to talk a little about Startup Chile.

In September, I saw an article in Techcrunch about the oporuntity to move my company to chile for six months. I filled out the website and four weeks later, they picked us for the program. When I arrived, I didn't know much about the program, only that I would be able to work on my company in another location and have a grant. The opportunity to avoid a Wisconsin winter was only an added bonus.

Now, six months later, my time in Chile is coming to an end. I can say that these six months were some of the best months of my life. We made a lot of progress on Entrustet, but more than that, we made good friends with all of the entrepreneurs in the program. We were connected into the Chilean entrepreneurship network and we made friends with Chileans inside and outside of the program.

Now, I want to talk a little about the program. Like Jean said, Startup Chile is a startup in it's own right and it's growing really fast. 100 team are going to arrive in the next two months. I want to thank all of the people in the government because without your permission, this innovative program never would have been successful. I want to say thanks to all of the people who work in Start-Up Chile.

This program is very special. I believe that many people, especially Chileans, don't understand this. When I talk to my friends about the program, they say to me "If Chile can do it, other countries can." But in reality, it's not the case. This type of program would never had happened in the US or Europe. The program is the most innovative government program I've seen in my life and every Chilean should be proud.

You've done something amazing and it's the start of something incredible. I want to see how the program and Chilean entrepreneurship grows in the next year. I want to end by thanking my startup friends, Startup Chile and every person who supported the program. Thank you.

Made in the USA
Middletown, DE
15 July 2018